ALMOST THERE, ALMOST

**THE MANY FACES OF
SYLVIA TRAYMORE MORRISON**

To Joan,

Sending love.

Love –

Sly. Tray Morrison
4/28/2012

This book product is available at special quality discounts for bulk purchase for sales promotions, premiums, fundraising, and educational needs. For details, write Almost There, Almost, 609 Clovis Avenue, Capitol Heights, MD 20743 or telephone (202) 506-3895.

Almost There Almost…The Many Faces of Sylvia Traymore Morrison

This book or parts thereof may not be reproduced in any form, stored in a retrieval system, or transmitted in any form by any means – electronic, mechanical, photocopy recording, or otherwise – without prior written permission of the author, except as provided by the United States of America copyright law.

Photos by Y&D Photography

Copyright © 2000 by Sylvia Traymore Morrison
All rights reserved

Morrison, Sylvia Traymore
Almost There Almost…The Many Faces of Sylvia Traymore Morrison
ISBN No. 9781453796573

Printed in the United States of America

This page is appearing in your book because you are the holder of one of the first 1,000 copies, a collector's item.

It has not been touched by any editors, ghost writers, publishers or co-writers. You are holding an original straight from my heart to you. Once the 1,000th copy is sold this page will be removed and some of the contents possibly changed. I hope you won't mind the typos or incorrect grammar. This was written all by me and I'm thanking God for each and every moment.

Thank you for your support.

Dear God:

Thank you for your awesomeness. Thank you for giving me the courage to put this book on paper. Thank you for pulling me through these trials and tribulations. Thank you for giving me a gift that I can share with the world. Thank you also for allowing me to finally wake me up to the realization of just how magnificent life is as a result of your mercy. Thank you. You know what Lord? You rock!

For Jasmin and Michelle:

Thank you for allowing me to live, and live with passion. I'm so blessed to have you in my life. You just don't know. I love you.

TABLE OF CONTENTS

Page

FOREWORD	2
INTRODUCTION	4
THE BEATING – OUCH!	5
POOCHIE – SISTER/SISTER!	8
DADDY – HE'S THE MAN!	9
BIG BETTY DON'T PLAY	12
THE HOUSE AND THE RATS AND WHATEVER ELSE	14
CIGARETTES – NOT SO TASTY	16
ANOTHER ONE BITES THE DUST	18
THE FINGER – WHY THE DOG?	22
SCHOOL – YAY!	24
THE MUSIC	27
THE JAZZ MAN	29
HIGH ON SCHOOL	31
THE HOMECOMING	34
THE TALENT SHOW	36
GOING PROFESSIONAL	38
COLLEGE AND NIGHTCLUBS?	39
SPELMAN	41
THE PAGEANTS	44
THE AIRLINES	51
THE NATIONALS	54

TABLE OF CONTENTS
(continued)

Page

THE MURDER	57
EUROPE	59
REDD FOXX	63
HOLLYWOOD AND SEX? FOR REAL?	68
DADDY 2	71
MA 2	73
THE CAR	76
SHEBAH	79
LARRY	88
THE ROAST	97
SATURDAY NIGHT LIVE	99
THE ABORTION	103
THE NIGHTCLUBS	111
THE CARTER BARON – MELBA MOORE	113
CHAKA KAHN	115
PARKWOOD	118
THAT DEVIL AIN'T NO JOKE	120
BACK TO SAN ANTONIO	123
WHITNEY INTRO	125
STAR SEARCH	128
WHITNEY 2	130
GOING BACK	138
CURTIS	144

TABLE OF CONTENTS
(continued)

	Page
PEACE	149
THE MARRIAGE AND THE BABY	151
HIV/AIDS	159
MY CHANCE - I CAN GET OUT NOW	170
A NEW LOOK	173
2003 – THE CALL	185
SUPERIOR COURT OF THE DISTRICT OF COLUMBIA	187
BACK TO BACK IN THE DAY	190
THE FINAL DIVORCE	195
THE ACCIDENT	200
COMING BACK	210

FOREWORD

When I was asked to write the foreword to this book my heart literally skipped a couple of beats. Thinking back to that initial reaction I realize now that I was intimidated. How could I do it justice and was I worthy of such a high honor? How was a formerly diagnosed 'uneducable' child, born and raised in the asphalt jungle of the first black publicly assisted housing project in America, chosen to write the foreword to one of the most important books ever written? How could an eighth-grade drop-out, ex heroin addict and former deliberate consumer of Federal Government Adjudication Services rise to such literary heights?

I don't know if I can answer those questions but I do know that as soon as I met the incomparable Sylvia Traymore Morrison in the spring of 2007 I had to be in her presence as often as possible. When I was awarded the privilege of performing on stage with her at the historic Black Repertory Theater in Oakland California and witnessed her receive (7) seven standing ovations, I knew that I had been gifted with a special blessing from God. I felt that my grandmother's prophesy of me one day rising up and doing something significant for black people, was finally coming true.

Still, my heart skipped a beat because I questioned my ability to frame this book in the light it deserves. I was however absolutely certain of this, "Almost There, Almost" reads like an Alice Walker novel with incredible speed, dazzling colorful metaphors, jazzy symphonic tones and an underlying melody that is both shocking and sobering at the same time.

The characters are as appealing as those provided by Walter Mosley and August Wilson; they are as gripping as those given to us by Dr. Maya Angelou and Toni Morrison. The manuscript is breathtaking in its scope, spanning some five decades of almost unbelievable escapades almost, and although it reads like a novel, it is actually the true life-story of one of the most remarkable human beings and one of the greatest entertainers that has ever graced this planet.

From the highs of airline stewardship and beauty pageants to the lows of an HIV death-sentence, an abusive spouse and crack houses, she takes us on an incredible journey. From opening for Whitney Houston in sold-out thirty thousand seat arenas, to standing in for Richard Pryor and hosting the roasting of the greatest of all time, Muhammad Ali, at the historic Apollo Theatre. It reads like a roller-coaster ride, filled with thrills, chills, kills and spills.

It is my humbled opinion that Sylvia Traymore Morrison should be lauded as a national treasure and that her story become required reading for anyone who is in need of motivation. This story outlines some of the most outlandish, extraordinary and yet, triumphant experiences anyone could imagine. They serve as inspiration to us all. You simply cannot read Almost There, Almost without being inspired.

Ty Gray-EL

INTRODUCTION

I always knew that the stage was someplace I'd live. I loved face and voice changes. I could sound like animals, cartoons and people. I was what people would identify later in life as an impressionist.

I remember being able to hear things that most people didn't. I could hear the flapping of a butterfly's wing. I could hear bees on their way to a flower. I could hear a watch ticking and I could hear cars outside in the early morning a block away having trouble starting. I could hear extra sounds from instruments in songs most people paid no attention to. I didn't just hear them. I could make the same sound. I could mimic some of the cartoon characters and stars I saw on television.

I loved how I could transfer sounds to myself and make the same sound down to the snores my father generated in his sleep. I could sound like the song of a cricket, the sound of the wind or the crack of a belt.

Having that gift would introduce me to the world. I would go from my front steps entertaining the kids in my neighborhood to traveling around the world entertaining the U.S. troops and thousands of people. I would meet some of the finest men and women in the world.

I'd like to share with you, some of the trials and tribulations I encountered as a result of seeking the stage. Yes, there was domestic violence, drugs, lifestyles and heartache, but it's been in my heart and soul no matter what the outcome of each trial or tribulation. I must now and always thank God for these awesome opportunities.

I love what this does for my spirit and the calm it brings to my heart. I pray that you are able to take a part of this story with you and hopefully, just once during this journey, be inspired to perhaps share your story too. God bless you.

THE BEATING – OUCH!

"Who set this house on fire?"

"Bunny."

"Who got the matches?"

"Bunny."

Ma and Daddy came out of the house bringing pans and trash cans of water. In those days, they rarely called the fire department or ambulance for fear of having to spend money they didn't have. Fortunately, they put the fire out with minimal damage to the inside of the house. The back looked like someone painted it black and I knew when Ma finished with me, my backside would be black too.

"You like playing with matches do you? I'ma teach you not to play with those damn matches anymore. Almost settin' the house on fire like you crazy. You must have lost your damn mind."

I was scared. Trembling. I thought I was going to die right there. My heart was beating at a rapid pace. I thought my eyes would pop out of my head. I got nauseous. I'm gonna die, I thought. Poochie told me to get the matches, her and that ol' Brenda Johnson from across the street.

I knew this would be a killer beating because I had seen her administer this type of whipping on my older sisters and brothers. It was my turn now and I was scared out of my wits. I couldn't even cry.

I saw the black leather belt hanging on the door knob. The buckle itself shined like it was blinking its eye at you. You could smell the leather. It was a heavy belt that belonged to Daddy, one he rarely wore because it was thick. He wore the thinner belt because it didn't weigh his clothes down like the one hanging.

It was waiting, like it was excited to be used, ready to slam up against anything. It instilled fear. Ma waved it in your face right before a beating and always talked about what foolishness she was not going to put up with before and during the beating.

She held me near the top of my arm close to my shoulder to make sure she had a good grip so that she could hit me exactly how and where she wanted too. She squeezed my arm tight. Too tight. It hurt.

Right before she struck, my wide eyes looked in hers. I knew I would be dead when the hit landed. Please don't Ma! Please don't. The first strike up against the backside of my little frail body came from the core of her strength. When the belt hit me, I thought someone threw a brick and cracked my back. It was a devastating hit, as if my body broke in two. I realized I was still alive and hoped she knew she almost killed me. The next hit felt like someone punched me in my back with their fist. The hits started coming one after the other. Oh my God. She was angry. With each strike she said a word.

"You! Like! Playin'! Wit! Matches! Do! You?!"

I started hollering because all of the hits felt hot. I was delirious. They kept coming. I cried and screamed to the top of my lungs. By this time, she let go of my arm and was slamming the belt down on me. Every time she hit me, I would grab the area she struck feeling the heat from the hit. You would have thought I was attacked by bees because I was reaching everywhere all over my body. She was busy screaming how dare I play with matches and set the house on fire.

The tears that spilled from my eyes met my runny nose which trickled down to my wet drooling mouth as a result of the uncontrollable crying. I must have looked like a monster. My voice became hoarse from screaming. My eyes were swelling from frowning and crying. When would it end? How much more? How much longer? Didn't she see I could not take a whipping like that? Was anybody going to stop her? Where was Daddy? Why didn't he rescue me? Somebody somewhere had to hear me. I was devastated, humiliated and hated every time she swung her arm in my direction.

The beating was over. She lifted me off my feet and slammed me on the bed like I was a little rag doll.

"If I ever catch you playing with matches again, I'll kill you. Do you understand me?"

In my hurt and anger with hardly any voice, I very quietly, softly and humbly answered.

"Yes Ma'am."

There was nothing I could do but whimper and cry. Welts, the size of long little earth worms were all over my body as if I was a piece of artwork. My face hurt, my arms were burning, my legs were lifeless and my whole body ached. I laid in the bed awake all through the night. One thing for sure, I would never play with matches again. I never forgot that whipping especially since it took days for me to heal from my wounds, both outside my body and inside my heart.

POOCHIE – SISTER/SISTER!

"Go get the matches Bunny."

Had I known going to get those matches would cause me a horrible beating, I would have never done it. I was 5 years old.

I didn't want to get the matches but I did everything Poochie told me. She was only a year older than me but still my older sister. She was shorter and people often joked that we looked like Laurel and Hardy, a comedy twosome from back in the day.

She was a cute little girl with raised eyebrows as if she was surprised about something. She was on the chubby side with a round face, a semi-boxed forehead which made room for her deep set nose, that was almost pointed but round at the same time. Her jaws sagged a bit in a unique cutie pie way, just enough to make her eyes bigger. She was like an older version of the young Raven from the Cosby Show. She didn't smile often, she out right laughed at almost everything. When she laughed, you laughed with her because it was infectious!

When she said go get the matches I felt like I had to. Plus, Brenda Johnson, our neighbor from across the street, was standing right there looking at me with those mean ol' wicked eyes. Her face was sunken at the cheeks as if she had not eaten for days. Her hair appeared to be undone with pieces of it sticking out all over the place, like a porcupine. She always looked sad. I never saw her smile. Her arms were skinny but moved quickly in brawls. She had no problem punching you first to start a fight. No one wanted a confrontation with her. She didn't care who she fought, except for Poochie.

I don't know why Poochie wanted to play with her but she did and since I was the younger sister, I played with her too.

DADDY – HE'S THE MAN!

When I was born, Daddy said I looked just like a rabbit because of my pug nose and funny ears. I use to squeeze my nose just like a rabbit so he wanted to name me Cottontails. My oldest sister Jerry, a big "ain't scared of nobody and nothing" type person and would fight you quick, saved me saying if I looked that much like a rabbit, call me something like Bunny but don't curse me with Cottontails.

My father, John, was a handsome man with brownish red skin, more brown than red. He had pure white hair and was probably one of the most handsome men I had ever seen. He was about 5'9" and thin with sharp features. His nose was mildly pointed and his cheek bones stood proudly on top of his jaws. His eyes were kind and stern at the same time. They were dark and he could look at you and not look at you. He had the look of a bad boy but carried the character of a man, who rarely smiled. His looks put you in the mind of Denzel Washington and a young Billie Dee Williams combined. As he got older he put me in the mind of Morgan Freeman. I could see how he charmed my mother when they first met. His posture appeared perfect and everything about him was charismatic including his walk. He stepped slow but strong. Because he was extremely thin, yet in shape, his clothes almost fit him like the soldier he was. He was proud to have been in the U.S. Army. Daddy had plenty of swag.

He was a quiet man who never bothered a soul unless he was drinking and then whatever he said or did was in the spirit of fun. I admired him and never let his drinking disturb me. I could see past the drinking and knew from stories I'd heard that he had been through hell in his life. Two wars and a tough upbringing made him older than his years. He was 12 years old when his hair turned pure white.

When I was maybe 6 or 7 years old, I remember my father telling my mother to call the police because he had just shot a man. In the 1950s, guns were not as popular in households as they are today. I vaguely remember the story but I do remember hearing about the neighborhood bully at the bar where my father frequented on paydays. He was a big guy they described and kind of looked like the cartoon character Popeye, for those of you who know Popeye, but heavier in places where the cartoon character was thin. His arms were thick but tiny at the bend near the elbow. He had a big chest and a tiny waist with muscular legs and big feet. He also had big teeth and busy eyebrows. The guy, from what I heard, had a heavy, deep voice, a huge, loud laugh and practically ran things in that particular part of the neighborhood. Apparently, he was showing off in front of everyone and would not stop. He was screaming at Daddy trying to make him the butt of his jokes. "Get yo ass out of here mf'er. When I say something, I mean it!"

They say Daddy got in his car, drove out to Virginia, bought a gun and went back to the bar. When the guy started his ranting again, Daddy politely asked the guy to leave him alone. This back and forth must have gone on for a few minutes until Daddy told the guy he didn't want any trouble. When the guy grabbed him it was over. Daddy pulled out his gun, shot him, injuring him. From that day forward, it was a different story when John Morrison showed up.

I would sometimes tease him saying "You must have thought you were in the wild, wild, west, huh?" He never responded but I knew he was okay with it. After all, I was Daddy's girl.

As he got older, his favorite pastime was sitting in front of the television and smoking his Camel cigarettes, one after the other. He rarely talked and when he did, it was usually a lesson of some sort, be it history, geography or old timey sayings. His favorite quotation was "He who knows not and knows not he knows not: he is a fool - shun him. He who knows not and knows he knows not: he is simple - teach him. He who knows and knows not he knows: he is asleep - wake him. He who knows and knows he knows: he is wise - follow him."

Daddy would say things and make me think about it for days. He took time to explain whatever I asked. If he didn't know an answer, he would find it. I thought he was king of the world.

He dropped out of school in the 8th grade to help his mother on the farm in the back hills of North Carolina in order to help take care of his two little brothers, considering his father died when he was young.

He indirectly educated himself while serving in the U.S. Army, learning to speak fluent French while in France, some Spanish and a good bit of German during his travels. Had he been able to get a formal education, I believe he would have easily been a lawyer or a doctor.

Daddy could tap dance too. He learned to tap from Bill "Bojangles" Robinson. Every once in a while he would treat us to one of his dances and I never understood why he wasn't professional. He was awesome.

His youngest brother, Uncle Tom, who I believe was the son of a White man because of his color and straight Black hair, was born with handicapped feet. While walking forward, Uncle Tom's feet faced backward. He is the only person I have ever seen with that type of handicap. The thing I remember most about Uncle Tom, other than his feet, is that he wore suspenders on his pants. I never saw him without them.

My heart aches when I meet women who never really knew their father. Dads are incredible in my opinion. I know mine was.

BIG BETTY DON'T PLAY

Betty Mae Morrison had 6 children, 4 girls and 2 boys - me the youngest. Today, I try to imagine what would have happened had she been forced to take us to daycare. It is almost laughable when I think about it. If you saw my mother, you would understand. She had the biggest hands on any woman I have ever seen. If she hit you with one of them, you were going down. They called her Big Betty.

She must have been a real live beauty in her youth. Daddy said her hair was coal black, silky and long.

"She looked like a satin doll. Lean, with golden colored skin and a sexy demeanor." We would give him a look like "are you serious? Ma? Sexy?"

"Your mother had perfect skin and eyes that were so mysterious and dark she could look at you and stop you in your tracks."

Her forehead was box shaped with a thick and full hairline. Her lips were small and unless she smiled you almost could not see them. Her nose was centered perfectly and matched everything else on her face. Her jawline sat high near her eyes and to look at her profile you would think of a young Alicia Keys. To Daddy, no one was more gorgeous. By the time I could make assessments of how she looked, I was older. She was 5'8" tall and weighed about 225 pounds.

She allowed us to brush her hair sometimes. She would let it fall down her back. We admired it. That is one of my fondest memories of her. She never hugged us or verbally said it but we somehow knew she loved us.

She stayed home while Daddy worked whenever, however, and whatever. She demanded respect, good behavior and quiet. There was no talking back, answering any question if you weren't asked and definitely no strange looks. That was cause for an immediate slap upside the head. I don't know where she got the energy but she was always up for a good "you gonna get a whipping, where's my belt?" mood. If she called your name, you'd better answer the first time because if she had to get up out of her chair to come looking for you, you'd better have a good alibi as to why you didn't answer the first time. Big Betty did not play.

THE HOUSE AND THE RATS AND WHATEVER ELSE

In the 1950s we lived in downtown Washington, DC. You could walk from our house at 1617 Corcoran Street, NW to the corner and see the White House which was about 12 blocks away. To think that we were that close to the White House and lived like we did baffled me for a long time.

Our house was small and old, heated by a steel stove that burned wood and coal. It was Peter, my brother's responsibility to shovel the coal during the winter months. Peter was quiet, never had much to say. He was light skinned and a target for the neighborhood guys because for whatever reason they associated light skin with weakness. Fortunately, he could fight. He was about 5 feet 1 or 2 inches tall and still growing. You could see hints of gray in his hair. He was a light skinned version of Daddy.

The green bin that sat up against the back of our house was old but sturdy. It must have been about 5 feet long and 5 feet wide and was the home for lots of rats. I feel sorry when I think of Peter and the rats jumping out of the bin when he opened it. He always ignored them and never complained. A lot of people would have had some kind of attack. Rats in our neighborhood were common.

One night during a heavy rain, I guess the rats decided to move into Daddy's old broken down Chevy because the bin was filling with water. It was a sight to see when Daddy decided to repair the engine. He had to almost run when he opened the hood. The rats were running and jumping everywhere.

Our house always seemed cold in the winter. We were forced to find ways to cover the cracks under the doors and holes in the windows. We used blankets, towels, old clothes or whatever we could find to block the wind from coming inside. There were 3 bedrooms. Four of us were in one of the bedrooms.

In the summer months, air conditioning was unheard of. We had one fan in the window in Momma's bedroom that sometimes blew in hot air from outside. Everyone crowded in her room to get air until it was time to go to bed. We suffered in the sometimes sweltering 90+ degree heat.

All of our clothes were washed by hand or on a washing board. As I got older, someone gave us an old washing machine, nothing like the washing machines today. There were no time mechanisms just an off and on button. Once the wash cycle completed, you had to refill the bin with water. The clothes had to be hand fed through the wringer, which sat on top of the washer, looking like two baking rack pins put together.

We didn't have a dryer either, but we, as well as our neighbors, hung clothes on clothes lines made out of rope. I cannot tell you how many times my friends and I took the rope down to play double dutch.

Food in our household was almost considered a luxury. Most mornings we ate cereal and many nights we ate pinto beans with homemade biscuits. We ate a lot of government issued food too. Cheese, powdered eggs and powdered milk and strange meat in a can that was supposed to be spam, was what we got at least once a month. In the 1950's food and homeless shelters were unheard of.

There was one black and white television set in our house. No one in our neighborhood had a color television yet. In order to watch TV for 15 minutes we had to deposit a quarter in a box on the back of it. That was the only way we could afford the luxury of a television. There were only four channels on television, channel 4(NBC), 5 (WTTG), 7 (ABC) and 9 (CBS).

CIGARETTES – NOT SO TASTY

Ma had a way of disciplining you that most people would certainly not approve of these days and times. She could care less what anyone thought and used her way at any cost. Teaching us to not want to smoke cigarettes was interesting and certainly not my choice of discipline but she got results.

Ma went downstairs but forgot that she left a burning cigarette in the ashtray in her bedroom. Poochie and I saw the cigarette burning and both decided to not let the cigarette waste but to take a drag. Not thinking anything was wrong, considering we saw both our parents smoking all of the time, we proceeded downstairs with the lit cigarette to smoke with our mother. Ma couldn't believe her eyes when she saw us coming down the steps.

"Oh, you like to smoke?"

"Yes ma'am" we both said at the same time.

"Go upstairs and get the carton of cigarettes from out of my top drawer."

We ran up the stairs excited she was going to smoke and socialize with us.

She opened a new pack giving us each our own cigarette. Poochie and I looked at each other with delight because we felt so grown. We finished the first cigarette. She gave us another one. I thought that was so nice of her. By the third cigarette, my mouth was dry and started tasting nasty.

"Smoke another one" she instructed us.

We obeyed but made faces at the nastiness of the smoke and started feeling sick. I was almost at a vomiting point. I had enough of those cigarettes and rejected mine. Poochie tried to be brave and smoked hers but midway through obviously had enough.

"I SAID SMOKE ANOTHER ONE!"

That voice, that strong, loud, voice. It was the "I mean business" voice. Then she said them – the worse words in the world at that moment.

"I said smoke the cigarette. If you don't smoke it, eat it."

Eat it? For real? Who eats cigarettes? There we were, chewing on the cigarettes. Scared and confused to death.

She made us eat the cigarette until we couldn't eat any more. We both got sick, and threw up all over the place. Ma knew that she would never have to worry about us smoking cigarettes again.

ANOTHER ONE BITES THE DUST

Ma's father died when she was 7 years old. Being the youngest of 14 children, 7 of whom passed for white, she and my grandmother, a White woman, left Virginia for Washington, D.C. to make a better life.

Several of my aunts had the middle name Mae. My mother was Betty Mae, there were her sisters Maude Mae, Mamie Mae, Hester Mae and then there was Mary Lou. Those are the only aunts that I remember having met out of the 14 children from Ma's side of the family. The others either died before I was born or chose not to come around for fear of exposing that they were in fact not White.

Ma was 11 years old when her mother died.

She stayed with a foster family who put her through high school and registered her for Howard University. She met a man named George Diggs. That affair produced my oldest sister, Geraldine, who we called Jerry. I know. I've been trying to figure for years how we spelled Jerry with a J instead of a G.

Ma found a job with a woman and was able to live free in exchange for helping around the house. The house was located on 17th & Corcoran Street in NW Washington, DC, one block away from where I grew up.

Ma met Daddy in that neighborhood and after they hooked up, they had my sister Johnnie Mae (there's that Mae again) whom we call Chubby. There's a picture that Momma kept of Chubby when she was about 3 years old. Warner Brothers did head shots of her because she was the spitting image of a Black Shirley Temple or as they referred to it, "a colored Shirley Temple."

While my father was in the Army, Ma gave birth to another brother Howard whom we call Jacky. After his return home from overseas they had my brother John, Jr., (Peter) and of course Poochie and me. Poochie's real name is Patricia.

Daddy was a disciplinarian as well. He whipped me once in my life.

It happened on a summer evening while we were living on Corcoran Street in a house next door to the house I described for you earlier in downtown D.C.

Mine and Poochie's favorite summer past time was catching what we called lightening bugs while most other people refer to them as fireflies. The problem with catching the bugs was, we had no trees or grass and the only place to catch them was around the corner on 16th Street. Remember, the White House was only blocks away. 16th Street was beautiful with all kinds of fancy cars and greenery. We didn't care about any of that. The important thing was the bugs.

We asked Daddy if we could to the corner to catch the bugs. "You can go around the corner, but whatever you do, DO NOT cross 16th Street under any circumstances."

He said that because, 16th Street, although beautiful, was dangerous and many people had been killed there. He repeated that we should NOT CROSS it and he meant it.

Disappointed there was not one bug on our side of the street, we stood there and watched all of the beautiful lightening bugs on the other side of 16th Street. Poochie came up with an idea.

"You catch bugs better than me. Run across the street, catch the bugs and bring them back! I'll watch out for Daddy."

"Oh no, Daddy's not gonna catch me across that street. He said DO NOT CROSS 16th Street."

She assured me that she would watch out and if I heard her screaming my name, just run back across the street. I was convinced.

As soon as I crossed the street, I had no idea that Daddy was on his way to see how we were doing and if we were obedient. Poochie had no idea either. The only thing I could hear was her mouth going 100 miles an hour - scared to death. "I told her not to go across that street, but she went anyway. There she is - right there."

What? She didn't scream my name? She didn't give me any warning? I saw him waiting to cross the street to come get me. Daddy had the kill look in his eyes.

His belt was different from Ma's. It was brown and thin but sharp. "Perfect for a beating" my brothers and sisters would say. The minute he got me across the street, he had taken off the belt and started whipping me. I could hear the sound of the belt coming every time the belt slammed across my head and back. One time the belt ripped across my face slapping into my eyes. After that, I didn't know what to expect because I could just barely see. The belt found the bottom of my legs. It felt as if hot irons were ripping through them. My arms felt like hot needles were sticking them. I thought my skin was being ripped from my body. I believed it was the worse whipping I ever had, even more so than the whipping I got for helping to set the back of the house on fire, not because it was so physical, but because it came from Daddy and I was his girl. It broke my spirit and my heart and also broke my skin causing blood to ooze out of some of the welts.

He whipped me all the way home. People were in their yards watching as I was screaming coming from the corner. Nobody breathed a word. As far as they were concerned, I did something wrong and was being punished rightfully.

I never disobeyed Daddy again, for fear of getting another one. I didn't talk to anyone for two days after that beating. Poochie didn't get a whipping - she didn't cross the street. Today, when we talk about that incident, she rarely shares because she believed she caused me to get a beating that no human in the world deserved.

I got 3 whippings in my life. The 3rd and final whipping ended up being a spoof. Poochie, Peter and I were told to go to bed. We didn't feel like it so we started playing in our room being disobedient jumping around on the furniture and screaming loud. My mother hollered up the steps that she would be right up as soon as she got the belt.

I wasn't having it. I didn't feel like crying my eyes out so I put all of my doll baby dishes in my underwear so that when the belt struck I wouldn't feel it. I don't know what made me think she wouldn't see the dishes. It worked out because when she struck me and realized what I'd done, she laughed herself silly and broke the mood of a whipping.

THE FINGER – WHY THE DOG?

Ma demanded we finish our chores after school which took a couple of hours. Sometimes it was dark by the time we finished, meaning we couldn't go outside. The times we could go out we made up games like baseball in the alley, hopscotch on the sidewalk and endless double-dutch jumping with 3 or more girls. We played hand/rhyme games, front step games and anything that came to our imagination.

Chores for the girls consisted of cleaning the kitchen countertops, washing and drying and putting the dishes away, mopping the kitchen floor, dusting all of the furniture in the living and dining rooms, wiping down the steps, sweeping the floor of each room in the house, polishing the furniture, emptying the trash, scrubbing the tub, mopping the bathroom floor, scouring the bathroom, and anything else Momma could think of. This was all daily routine. Daddy showed us how to make a bed army style and I promised myself that when I grew up I would hire a housekeeper.

In our household we almost never, ever visited the doctor or the dentist. If the school didn't provide services, you didn't get any.

I got chased by a dog, ran down the street and fell up a set of steps, crashing into the concrete breaking the ring finger on my right hand. The pain was excruciating but I couldn't tell Ma because I was not supposed to leave the front yard. She said do not leave the yard and that's what she meant. I was afraid of the dog and afraid of Ma but at that particular moment, the dog ruled and I ran out of the yard. It was just my luck to fall and hurt myself.

After 2 days of pain, I showed Ma the ugly finger. She shoved it off as if it would go away. A day or so later, she saw how swollen the finger was and decided to take me to the emergency room. It was broken. They splintered it and said I had to come back in 6 weeks. Ma fixed it. It was bad enough we had a hospital bill for going to the hospital in the first place. The hospital never saw us again.

There was also the time that I ran into a telephone pole that was full of rusted nails. While out back in the alley playing with my friends, I was running with my head turned and didn't see the pole. By the time I turned around I ran smack dab into the pole and hit my face into one of the nails causing it to penetrate just above my eye near my brow, the scar of which I still sport today. The blood was unbelievable and instead of taking me to the hospital Daddy attended to it by pouring alcohol into and around the wound. There is nothing I can tell you about the pain. It was awful but homemade remedies outweighed going to the hospital. There was no money for treatment and we never heard of medical insurance.

SCHOOL – YAY!

My first grade teacher, Ms. Daily, a charming short, "don't know if she's Black or White" woman allowed me to do special projects in class because I generally finished my work ahead of everyone.

Every month, a classroom was responsible for a presentation to the school. At that time, we were allowed prayer in school. Ms. Daily told me to go home and memorize the first 5 verses of Genesis, the first book in the Bible. I was excited but wondered why she picked me? What made her decide that I deserved this honor? I did exactly what she told me and the day arrived.

Ms. Daily walked up to the front of the auditorium, welcomed everyone and instructed me to come forward. She leaned down to my ear and whispered.

"I want you to do this just like you did in rehearsal, okay?"

"Yes m'am."

Say your part loud and clear. I know you'll do just fine. And Sylvia? I'm so proud of you."

"Thank you Ms. Daily."

I almost had tears in my eyes when she said that. Everyone's eyes were on me. When I finished the verses, totally memorized and well spoken, the audience stood up on their feet. I thought they were about to leave but they applauded for a very long time. I didn't know what to do. Ms. Daily was so proud she smiled and hugged me for I don't know how long.

By the time I got to the third grade I auditioned for the role of the mother for our classroom play. I liked the intensity of people watching while I auditioned. They made interesting faces. Another girl beat me out. Not only did she physically look the part, she was clearly the better actress. I was named her understudy.

The teacher asked if I wanted to be the Mistress of Ceremonies because she felt no way could I just not do anything. She told me to also lead the school in the National Anthem. No student had done that.

During rehearsals, she would often call other teachers to come watch. I honestly can't express to you how delighted I was when they were all standing there looking and whispering. I spoke loud. My words were clear and I used my hands to express how I felt. When I said "WELCOME" I meant it, assuring my make-believe audience that they were in for a treat.

I had a powerful speaking voice, probably from all that crying and whooping and hollering I did when I got my whippings. I didn't need a microphone. I could imitate many of the teachers and the principal as well. People would say "do Mr. Jackson" or do so and so. I couldn't wait for the day of the play. My teacher was more excited than me.

I secretly wished that Ma would come but her attitude was it might cost money and she didn't want any parts of it. To my surprise, she walked in the auditorium the day of the play! I was proud to see her because that was the first time I could ever remember her coming to our school for anything other than to whip one of us in front of the class.

When I had the attention of every single person in the auditorium, I stretched my arms, raised my hands for everyone to sing the national anthem in unison and led the entire school as if Mozart himself was sitting there watching. My arms flowed and don't ask me how, but I knew how to make the audience follow my instructions. Their eyes were directly on me. I saw people smiling, whispering to each other that they couldn't believe what I was doing. You could tell by their expression they were thinking who taught this child how to do this? I was only 8 years old.

At the end, our principal spoke about my leadership. He raved about the performance.

"Wasn't Sylvia wonderful? I don't think I've ever seen anything like this!"

Ma never said whether she liked it or not. I never knew what she thought and was too afraid to ask. My teacher, on the other hand, was extremely proud and let me know as did several others.

The remainder of my elementary school years, I was in a production, usually in the lead role. I was not afraid to perform and the teachers knew it.

Saturday mornings I spent time with the area kids calling myself the teacher. There were many large families on my block. We had the Johnsons, the Clairs, the Carters, the Hamiltons, the Jennings, the Taylors, the Newmans and the Norris's. Baby Ray, whose real name was Delores Clair was my best friend in the world. The Clairs had a house full of kids and all of the kids on the block and in the surrounding neighborhood loved being friends with the Clairs. Whenever I went to their house their mother seemed to always be cooking and the aroma of her southern style was mesmerizing.

Almost each family had anywhere from 4-11 kids and some of those kids had their own kids making for a lot of children on the block. Play school on Corcoran Street was a dream comes true for me, especially since I would make the kids laugh imitating people. The parents loved that I was a play teacher because it kept them from having to worry about what their kids were doing.

THE MUSIC

I found solitude at a place called the Uplift House which was around the corner from where we lived at 1502 Q Street, NW. There were all types of arts and crafts available for children. There was a piano that I found fascinating. I could touch the different keys and after a while sing some of the songs I learned in school.

One summer, a group of White college students from Iowa came to Washington in a summer job program and worked with us. They were encouraging and told us daily what a wonderful job we were doing. They were kind too. We didn't hear White people talk often and their choice of words sounded funny compared to ours. I started mimicking how they talked and all of the kids laughed.

One of the instructors who watched and listened to me at the piano explained that I was playing by ear. She suggested that I get my parents to arrange for me to take piano lessons. Yeah right. I couldn't dare tell my mother that. She must have seen something in my face because she sat down and told me she would teach me everything she knew about the piano.

She started with middle C and after a while I was in heaven having learned a little about the piano. I can't remember her name, but for the next 4 weeks she worked with me.

She went back to Grinnell College in Iowa and wrote me a letter wanting to know how my piano lessons were coming. I regret not ever writing back. Those few piano lessons were invaluable and her kindness generated a kindness in me to do the same.

Speaking of pianos, Ma's sister who lived in Waukegan, Illinois, Aunt Mary Lou knew how much I loved the piano. She put in her will that should she die before me, she wanted me to have her piano. When she died, it was shipped to me from Illinois soon afterwards. I believe that part of my interest in the arts may have come from both sides of the family considering Daddy was such a tap dancer and Aunt Mary Lou was a wonderful piano player.

By the time I got to middle school I thought I was a musical genius until I ran into some real musicians.

I met up with Toni, Wanda and Gail in the 7th grade. They were attractive, smart and talented. The four of us quickly became friends.

Toni and Gail played the violin and were good. I decided to sign up to learn how to play the violin, hoping my lessons from the piano would help. Me - living in one of the dungiest parts of the ghetto, carrying a big ol' giant violin in its case, home every day.

There was no encouragement or excitement in my house about my new venture, only complaints, except for Ma and she didn't care one way or the other. She allowed me to pluck and scratch on my violin all day. I became good enough to be in the school concert.

We sounded a hot mess and I thought the school orchestra was good but nobody was banging on the doors asking us to perform. They did bang when they heard me, Gail and Toni sing. We were just messing around harmonizing when we realized we sounded pretty good. We formed our own group.

THE JAZZ MAN

Our singing group was invited to the Mayor's office to sing for some jazz guy who was getting a key to the city for the wonderful work he did in jazz. Kids in my neighborhood didn't listen to jazz so we had no idea who we were going to see, but whoever this guy was, they were filming the event to be shown on the news that night.

While waiting for our turn to entertain, I saw a man who reminded me of one of Daddy's friends. He looked awfully familiar, like one of the around the way older men. I walked up to him and started a conversation wanting to know if he, in fact, knew my father.

"Excuse me - Do you know a man named John Morrison?"

"Who?"

"John Morrison?"

"I don't know. Who is he?"

"He's my father. You look so familiar like somebody he knows. You two even look like you could be related."

"I don't know. We probably do know each other. Or since we look so much alike maybe he's my long lost cousin. Where do you live?"

"We live on 16th and Corcoran Street. I don't know, but you sure look familiar. You don't hang out on 17th & Corcoran Street?"

He then casually revealed who he was.

"I may have. But I tell you what. Tell your father that Duke Ellington said hello and ask him if we are long lost cousins."

"Ok. I will. What's your name again?"

"Duke Ellington."

We chatted a little more about why I was there, me trying to impress him telling him we were there for some famous jazz guy and before I knew it, a bunch of people rushed him out of the room. I thought no more about him or our conversation because we never got to sing for whoever the famous jazz guy was that night. There was not enough time so we left before he got the key to the city.

A little later that night, I saw the guy I spoke with earlier on TV and it was him! I called Daddy in the room and told him what happened.

"He said his name was Duke something. Is he some kind of star?"

"The guy you were talking to is Duke Ellington, one of the best big band leaders ever - the best that ever did it. Did you get his autograph?"

Autograph? I didn't even know he was somebody. This Mr. Duke Ellington and I talked like we were old friends. No, I didn't get the autograph, but I would hear his music later in life and thank God that I had the fortunate opportunity to meet one of the greatest people in the music business.

HIGH ON SCHOOL

By the time we got to Western High School, Toni, Gail and I were still singing together off and on. Western was having a talent show and I wanted to be in it so bad! Cheerleader tryouts were coming up and I had to be in that too.

I didn't make the cheerleading squad so I decided to run for homecoming queen. I don't know why because there was a short chance I would win. Fortunately, I easily won the eyes of one of the coolest guys in school. Edward "Radar" Jones.

Radar could have cared less that I didn't make the cheerleading squad. He liked me and made it clear to all of the fellas. He was definitely not my type. He was tall, skinny and loud and thought he was every girl's dream, which he was - I just didn't know it. Plus, he had big ears, which is why they called him Radar. He was forever pulling my hair, saying stuff, talking to me when I didn't want to talk, sitting with me at the games and pretty much getting on my last nerve. It wasn't until he focused his attention elsewhere that I recognized how charming he was. I began to see why all of the girls were crazy about him. I realized I liked his attention and the next thing I knew, he asked me "to go with him." I said yes and we became an item.

We talked on the phone (unbeknownst to Ma) laughed, played with each other at school and had a real no-sex relationship. After all, sex was nowhere in my thoughts, even when Ma decided to let me go on the one and only date she ever approved.

The condition of the date was I could go to the movies with Radar, if and only if Peter went with us. Ma figured if Peter went, there would be no chance of sneaking off. Little did she know, Peter and his girl (who later became his wife) went off to sit somewhere away from us. He was trying to get his own groove on.

I had never been on a date. The only thing I remember about the movie Cool Hand Luke is Paul Newman ate 50 eggs. Radar put his arm around me like it was normal and I thought I was going to die. My heart started racing, my eyes got big and I couldn't talk. Should I move his arm or just sit there? Should I put my arm around him too? Suppose Ma walked in and caught us?

I never saw any more of the movie. I felt like the most special girl in the world. The boy that stole my heart was sitting here in the movie theatre with his arm around my neck. He smelled good too.

Out of nowhere, he grabbed my face, turned me to him and kissed me. It was so awkward. I never kissed anybody. He was a pro. He juiced up his big ol' lips and placed them on my dry half chapped lips. I was embarrassed but didn't move. My body shut down. I kept my eyes closed because for one, my lips were a mess and I didn't want to look at him. I didn't know what in the world I was doing. Do I open my eyes and look at him? My hands were sweating. It felt like wind was blowing cool air on my lips because his big ol' lips were juicy and wet and wet mine. I sat there. He never said a word. Neither did I. The movie was over. I was in love.

We got up without saying a word. Had he said anything to me I wouldn't have been able to answer. My mind was completely blank. He kissed me! I just hoped I didn't stump my toe and look like a fool.

We found Peter and his girl and walked home. I must have dreamed about that date for the next 30 days. I couldn't wait for the next one. I was in love and it never occurred to me that almost every girl in the neighborhood was in love with him too. Simply put, Radar was a player.

One evening the word was out that he cheated on me and everyone was waiting on my reaction. How was I to know how to react? I never even had a boyfriend, much less been cheated on. I couldn't talk to Ma (please, she would have killed me) and Poochie didn't know what to do either so I just "quit" him. I was miserable. He played the role real good like it didn't bother him at all. He went on with his life. I was half dead from heartache. The first night was the most horrible. I couldn't eat a thing, couldn't sleep and didn't want to talk. My life was over. The only man I ever loved was gone off on the horizon.

It was my full intention to make up with him but I decided I'd wait on him to apologize, make up and maybe take me off into fantasy land.

I would go from being half dead to fully dead. I had no idea that he started seeing Toni. I was devastated, angry and hurt but never, ever let on. I couldn't let anybody see or know of my broken heart. But life for me, I thought, would never be the same.

As if that wasn't enough the properties on Corcoran Street were sold and we were forced to move. We heard about people uptown. The upper class, the bourgeois, the rich, the classy, etc. but never in my wildest dreams did I think we would actually move there.

In late 1968, while I was still in high school, we moved to 14th & Shepherd, NW in a nice, big 4 bedroom, 3 bathroom home completely different from the tiny 3 bedroom, 1 bathroom home we left. The rooms were huge, the landscape was fabulous and the people were nosey. They wanted to know everything about us to insure that we fit in but were a little disappointed to learn that my father was neither a lawyer nor my mother a school teacher. We upset the neighborhood by throwing a party the first week we were there to show our old friends our new house. We had one of those parties where it was too hot to stay inside so half the people hung outside of our house to get air. I believe half our neighbors fainted.

THE HOMECOMING

I was nominated to represent my homeroom for homecoming queen. I tied with the prettiest girl there. Radar was in our homeroom but absent the day of the vote. The next day the teacher asked for his vote. He played the whole day telling me that he voted for the other girl.

That afternoon, the winner was announced. I thanked him, because I knew I had been mean and he could have easily voted for the other girl.

"I hope you win."

I was still hurting from his union with Toni but sad that he was going in the hospital to have surgery on his ears. I won the title. It was a cold October day in 1969 and I had nothing to wear to the dance. Ma squeezed $45 out of the little money she had from her side hustle.

Of the $45, I had to get a dress, shoes, stockings, jewelry, makeup, and hair. The $29 dress, a purple mini, with tiny chains crisscrossing the front hugged at the waist and flared at the bottom, complimenting my skinny, 99 lbs. frame. I found the perfect $10 shoes to match. There was hardly any money left, but I saw the cutest $3 hat, forgetting I had to remove the hat in order to receive the crown for my head but I couldn't afford to get my hair done. I applied a little makeup I found in the house. The evening of the dance, I got dressed and received the stamp of approval from my family. I was nervous about my date because this would be the first time he and I would meet.

I was on the bus on my way home from school when I saw the finest, handsomest guy. He was standing right outside the pool room on 14th & T St., seven blocks from the famous Howard Theatre. A friend of mine, who knew almost everybody that lived in that area, knew exactly who I was talking about, or so I thought.

"That's Leonard Simms."

I asked if she would give him my number so I could invite him to the dance. He called and wanted to go.

Leonard appeared at my front door the night of the dance and oh my God! He was not the guy I saw the day I was on the bus. It was his brother Pee Wee I was talking about, but there was nothing I could do at that point.

Leonard was proud he was taking the Queen. We were leaving the house around 8:00 pm when Ma said I had to be back by 10. I estimated that by the time we got to the dance in Georgetown, it would be time to turn right back around to come home. I asked could we have a little more time, out of Leonard's ear shot because I didn't want him to hear. I was embarrassed enough as it was that she wanted me home in 2 hours. She gave me another hour.

We took a cab, me with my $29 dress, $10 shoes and $3 hat. While walking beside him, I was taller and in those days a good couple was a tall man and short woman so I kind of bent down while walking. I looked pretty silly doing that but I didn't care.

At the dance, I was crowded by people who were congratulating me. No sooner than I could get in the door good, Leonard was gone. He was spending most of his time with a girl he knew from Georgetown so I didn't see him the majority of the dance. I was busy trying to figure out what I was going to say or do when they called me on the stage. I was hoping I could perform something, which lately was always on my mind.

He was 21 years old and I was only 16. He rocked my world with his mature words which were "yeah man" and "that's slick." I was still trying to figure out what our group was going to do for the talent show.

THE TALENT SHOW

Five girls, who called themselves The Passions, took the stage. Each of those girls, in my opinion, appeared stuck up and snotty but confident. All 5 were attractive and could sing. They stepped like the Temptations and sounded like Smokey Robinson and the Miracles. They had a look of their own and range like Earth, Wind and Fire. The only thing they needed was a manager.

Two of the sisters in the group had to leave. The other 3 approached me and asked if I was interested. I said yes.

Eastern High School's talent show was coming up. The Passions and I rehearsed but there were complaints from them. "We use to do it like this" or "We should have found 2 girls instead of 1." They missed the two sisters that left and constantly compared me with them.

The night of Eastern High's talent show there was a lot of excitement especially since we were performing with the Choice Four. A couple of groups went on ahead of us, and then it was our time.

"PLEASE WELCOME TO THE STAGE - FROM WESTERN HIGH SCHOOL - THE PASSIONS!"

We stepped on stage to the Temptations' hit, Cloud Nine with our afros and matching psychedelic pantsuits, perfect for 1969. According to everyone backstage we looked good and the steps were tight! We were sounding like professionals and based on the applause, the audience loved us. We knew that we would not win first place, because Eastern was not going to let the only group who wasn't from their school take that spot. Besides they had some really good talent.

We won the third place trophy and were pleased especially since we were the only females in the competition. Darlene, one of the Passions started being nice. Originally from Dallas, Texas, she had a slight southern drawl. The guys loved her bow legs and she knew it. Darlene often talked in a sexy whisper until you got her wrong and then that southern tomboy came out. She didn't play. She also had a special way with people and I recognized that if she came in contact with you, more than likely she would win you over. Her spirit was wonderful.

Brenda was quiet and distant. All she wanted was for all of us to get the parts right, step properly and perform well. Not pressed for friendships, she wanted results. We did well and everybody in school was talking about us including the Dreams, who had a hit record "Don't Be Afraid, Do As I Say" and would later become Father's Children, the most popular group at Western High School and soon to become one of the most popular groups around.

Rona just wanted to be in the group.

GOING PROFESSIONAL

A disk jockey, which is what we called radio personalities back in the day, from WOL Radio (now owned by Cathy Hughes from Radio One) heard about us. They used names like Nighthawk and Youngblood.

Soul Poppa had connections in the entertainment industry both good and bad. He liked us and took us to meet with the Philadelphia Sound organization in hopes of getting a recording contract. He purchased most of our equipment and uniforms in addition to paying for all of our travels. He believed we were headed for stardom and hung in there with us. Our first professional engagement was at Constitution Hall.

Darlene went to Texas that 1969 Christmas holiday to see her family. She got married. We were devastated because she was clearly the best singer in the group. We had to find the right replacement. Shirley went to school with us and sounded like the leader of The Five Stairsteps. She joined. We practiced and came up with a respectable set but it just wasn't working. All of us had different schedules and agendas. We knew it was over. High school was almost over anyway. In the back of my heart I still had the desire to sing but I just didn't think I was strong enough to go solo.

Some people were going away to college, some were going to the military, some were getting jobs and some didn't know what they were doing. I applied to Grinnell College in Iowa inspired by the woman who befriended me at the Uplift House. I had not heard from Grinnell. I needed a miracle. I didn't know how, but when the time came I was determined to be on somebody's campus.

We bid our goodbyes, signed each other's year books and headed to our lives. It was sad. I loved high school and I still loved Leonard Simms too.

COLLEGE AND NIGHTCLUBS?

Ma's cousin managed to talk me into attending DC Teacher's College, which is called the University of the District of Columbia today. Ma heard us discussing it and was furious.

"Tell her you have to get a job and help the family. You can't go to college. Say thank you but no thank you."

I guess since Ma didn't work and Daddy was on disability, she expected her kids to get out of school, get a good job and help with the bills. She needed our help and didn't want any interference, especially somebody talking about going to college costing more money out of the household. As much as I wanted to go, I declined the college offer, got a good "gubment" job with the Treasury Department and decided I would be 18 the next year and go away to college. In the meantime, I took classes in the evening.

I got a call from a guy in SE Washington, DC asking if I would be interested in auditioning to perform for his buffet club called the Chef's Table located on Benning Road in the far NE section of Washington, DC, right off East Capitol Street. I was ecstatic because I had never done a solo performance so I accepted hoping I didn't make a fool of myself. He hired me on the spot with a pianist named Phil Stancil.

I must have been at the Chef's Table for about 2 weeks when the owner called me into his office. He proceeded to give me his critique.

"I really like what you bring and I think you are helping my club to grow. I like you so much I went out and got these for you."

He opened up a beautiful box that contained two fabulous dresses.

"I like you Sylvia and I'd like to call you mine."

Huh? Is he serious? I looked at him because I was so shocked I didn't even know how to answer him.

"Will you accept these from me?"

I didn't know what to say, so me with my old fashioned self came up with what I thought was a good answer.

"My mother told me that if you ever accept a gift from a man, he would expect something in return."

"Your mother is a smart woman."

I declined, left out that evening and never went back.

I wanted to go to Spelman ever since I heard my next door neighbor and a couple of his friends talking about their experiences at Morehouse, the brother school to Spelman. They were a year ahead of me, smart, skilled, rich and handsome.

The Morehouse guys and a few others who visited Washington in the summer each year right before school started were an exciting group and made going away to college seem like the best thing in the world. I wanted to get away from Ma's strict rules and away from Leonard too. I had to find out what was so dynamic about Morehouse and Spelman.

I landed another singing job at a place called Zanzibar's. Phil Stancil was on piano, Dave Yarborough, one of the District's finest jazz musicians (who also taught at Duke Ellington High School) was on sax, a drummer and bass formed a jazz band. They were awesome and I had no idea at the time that I was working with some of the greatest musicians in the country. I still couldn't figure out that I could actually sing for real because I was basically singing Jazz and didn't know that if you could sing Jazz you could sing almost anything.

SPELMAN

I received an acceptance letter from Spelman and couldn't sleep for 2 months thinking how I was going to Atlanta, Georgia! I worked a full time job from 8:30 am to 5:00 pm, went to D.C. Teachers in the evening from 6:00 pm to 9:00 pm. Left school and went to the club from 10:00 pm to 2:00 am to perform. Where I got the energy, I don't know but I did that for the rest of the time I was in DC.

Ma was angry at me wanting to go away and took no part in it. I went to the airport alone, got on the plane alone and paid for everything out of the money I saved. After all, I was going to a real big time Historically Black University.

In Atlanta I was dumbfounded. Where in the world was Spelman? Was it in the suburbs? Did I need to take a cab or could I take a bus? I saw a driver holding a sign that said "Spelman College."

I may not have had any support or help, but I had hope and I was determined. Besides, I already knew 2 of the hottest guys at Morehouse and was sure they would introduce me around.

I went to the main building where I was assigned a room in Manley Hall, an upper class dorm. I was a transfer student. Upper class. That was a new term for me. Upper class. I liked how that sounded.

My room was a storage room in the basement of Manley Hall made into a bedroom at the last minute because there were no other rooms available for transfer students. My roommate, who had already arrived and left back out, put her belongings on one side of the room. I was glad because I would not have known what to do.

When Regina walked in, I froze. She was tall, beautiful, confident, informed but most of all friendly and we hit it right off. I couldn't help but notice her dark features. Her hair was long and black and her eyebrows were thick and bushy. Her eyes always seemed squinted but charming. She was about 5'9, built like a racehorse and in good shape. She was a runner. She also had the prettiest smile but you could tell she was no nonsense. She was also a transfer student from Elizabeth City, NC.

Her father was a sergeant in the U.S. Marine Corps and her family traveled all over the world. I laughed to myself because my travels included the trip to Philadelphia with Soul Poppa and the Passions and the Atlantic City Boardwalk.

She had already checked out the campus and wanted to show me around. I thought to myself, wait until she finds out I know Howard and Sprint. When she did find out, she had no idea who a Howard or a Sprint were and quite frankly, could have cared less. Whenever we walked past guys, they stared.

"We're the new girls on the block. Guys come out like this every year to check on the new faces."

I learned a lot that day from Regina. I had been on campus a couple of days and was surprised that I had not heard one word from Howard or Sprint. I was a little embarrassed because I told most of the upper class girls I met that Howard was my next door neighbor and Sprint visited my house regularly. They questioned the validity of that because when I saw Howard and Sprint, they acted as if they didn't know me.

A lot of the girls at Spelman were from money and/or professionals. It was interesting that almost everybody on campus was smoking weed, cocaine and whatever else. They were always looking for a good connection. And sex? I swear they should have changed the name from Spelman College to Sex College. People had sex everyday all day, everywhere and anywhere. They were having sex in between classes, behind the cafeteria, outside of the dorms, in their rooms, the bathrooms, wherever they could find a spot. I laughed constantly at the heart of some of them.

I was not into drugs and was too busy trying to figure out what was happening on the night club scene and where I could get a job performing.

While sitting in the dorm's recreation room one of my dorm members was playing the piano and singing. I decided to sing along at her request. I don't know what hit me that day, but a new voice came out of my body. Students started gathering around wondering why I never let on that I had a voice like that but I didn't know where it came from either. One of the girls that heard me introduced me to two of her friends who happened to be local record producers. They gave me a tape with a song they wanted me to learn to cut a record. We never made it to the studio. I believe they may have lost the grant or studio they were working out of. They just disappeared. When I think about it now, they probably got caught up in all of those drugs and sexual activities taking place on the campus or maybe went to jail.

There was also a young woman who happened to be President of the Supremes Fan Club who was visiting the campus one weekend and heard me sing. "You are the next leader of the Supremes. I just know it! I believe they have someone slated, I think her name is Jean Terrell, but once they see you, they'll change their minds. I'll call you after I find out."

She called me back and said I was too young.

THE PAGEANTS

In 1972, after my first year at Spelman, I entered the Ms. Black DC pageant. Don't ask where I got the nerve because I don't know. I wanted to get on television and hopefully give my career a boost. There were over 100 applicants. It was exciting seeing all those girls ready to compete against each other. We all thought we were hot.

Contestants were singing, dancing or doing dramatic interpretations. I decided to do my version of the Ed Sullivan Show, the Oprah Winfrey of the 70's. His guests would include Jane Hathaway, secretary to Mr. Drysdale on the Beverly Hillbillies and Diana Ross, who was one of the biggest female singers at that time. I would close with a new act, Sylvia "Bunny" Morrison dancing to and singing "If I Had A Hammer" a song made popular by the late great Sam Cooke. It worked.

I made the first cut and the next thing I knew sponsors were coming from everywhere. Helena Darden said she and Vashti Spriggs wanted to sponsor me. They thought I was going to win the competition, go to the nationals and bring the title home so I said let's do it.

Ruth Turner and Marlene Daniels, two of the ladies chosen to work with us were former beauty pageant winners, or so I thought. They knew everything. Marlene was one of six Washington Redskinettes and everything about her spelled class.

NBC picked up the rights to the pageant. Dewey Hughes, a local producer for NBC, was in charge of the entire television production.

After he got a chance to see what the contestants were doing he asked if he could speak with me. I couldn't figure out what he wanted but guessed it had to be something good. He was a busy man.

"I think you have the pageant in the bag but you are weak in the bathing suit competition. You're too thin. You have to camouflage your body and hope the judges pay more attention to your swimsuit. Tell you what, go out and buy a bathing suit, I mean a really stunning one and bring me the bill. I don't care where you get it or what it costs. Go to Garfinckel's,

Woodies, Lord & Taylor or anywhere, I don't care. Just get it. You're going to win that contest, and they are going to love you in Indiana."

I don't know what made Dewey think that I could just go out and buy an expensive bathing suit. I had no money. Nobody in my family knew I was going to be in the contest and even if they did, couldn't afford to buy new clothes and bathing suits and all of that foolishness, as Ma would say. I never purchased the bathing suit.

The beauty in the pageant was Rasheeda Moore. Her family lived around the corner from me and was a first cousin to Toni. She had no real talent, but oh my goodness, she had looks and a body to die for. She was so pretty that everyone thought she would win the title on looks alone.

Another one of my good friends from the pageant was Moorean Baker. The Bakers made you feel at home. When I was invited out to California by Redd Foxx to audition to be a part of his team, on one of my return trips home, the Bakers gave me a party spearheaded by Moorean. It was the talk for weeks. She knew how to throw a party. From the day we met in high school, I knew she would do something special. She recently transitioned from a professor at Howard University's Dental School and is now courting a successful dental practice in Washington, DC.

Rona, my friend from the Passions, convinced me to tell my family about the pageant. I don't know why because Ma rarely went to any of my engagements. To my surprise, Momma and Daddy wanted tickets.

Everybody made a big deal out of the two of them dressing up. Daddy was the handsomest man there and Ma looked like a queen. It was the first time I had ever seen them together on a "date." Other than the graduations, Ma and Daddy never went out together.

I was confident in the talent area, but nervous about Dewey Hughes seeing that I had not bought a fabulous bathing suit like he suggested. The plain yellow bathing suit that Helena got me would have to do.

The program started with all of the contestants being lifted from under the stage at Howard University's Crampton Auditorium. I saw the huge crowd and felt right at home. Of the entire group of contestants, the judges were going to select 15 finalists.

Clint Holmes, our host, (who stars in Las Vegas) started calling names and my hands started sweating.

"Our 7th contestant to have a chance at becoming Ms. Black DC is, Rasheeda Moore."

Well, that was no surprise because we all knew she would get there. By no. 10, I was a little scared. They called the thirteenth contestant and I was just about dead. No. 14 was Moorean Baker. I felt like crying. I didn't make it?

My mother, father, sisters and friends were sitting out there. I felt sick.

"Our 15th and final contestant who will compete for the title of Miss Black District of Columbia is (drum roll) - Sylvia Morrison!"

I smiled so hard I could have screamed. Thank God! I made it! I was in the 15! I didn't care what happened after that. I made the cut!

Minnie Cohen, one of the contestants and probably the person I grew closest to didn't make the finals. She smiled and whispered in my ear "I hope you win." Minnie was such a sweetheart and I knew we would remain friends.

My composure was now together and I had a little confidence to boot, but I kept thinking how being no. 15 was scary. Everybody backstage kept saying they didn't know why I was worried. Moorean told me she figured they would save me for last. I just wish someone had told me.

People were practicing their talent and getting makeup redone backstage. You would have thought I was the official director/producer for the talent segment because almost everyone asked me for tips. Should I sing a false voice for this part; should I cut that part out of my dance; should I wear this scarf for my interpretation; and most importantly Valerie. She wrote a poem about drug addicts.

Drugs, mainly heroin, had become a big thing in the early 70s. People were dying and losing family members to that drug. I told Valerie that she had to somehow or another let the audience know that she wrote that poem herself and didn't get it out of a book.

"When you recite it, look people in the eye Val, take your time, make sure your words are clear, put depth in them, make people feel what you say, act it out! Deliver it. Make them want more."

She did. The audience loved her. They screamed, they shouted, they applauded. She was magnificent.

Rasheeda's talent portion of the competition was okay but she was beautiful and you didn't focus any attention to what she was doing. The makeup, outfit, regal beauty and her ability to capture an audience on her beauty alone was enchanting. At this point, I didn't know what to think. Everyone was doing well. It was as if magic appeared and each one of the top 15 improved overnight.

"Our final contestant is going to do a song, a dance and a dramatic interpretation. Please welcome Sylvia Morrison."

The place got quiet. Even backstage peopled stopped to watch.

I walked to the middle of the stage and opened by introducing Ed Sullivan. The audience applauded not only because I sounded exactly like him, they had never seen a Black woman doing impressions.

Ed introduced Jane Hathaway. I almost lost some of my time because the audience would not stop laughing. If you closed your eyes and listened, you would have thought Jane Hathaway was on that stage. He thanked Jane and introduced Diana Ross. They loved the impression of Diana Ross because I could I talk and sing exactly like her.

I could hardly hear myself by the time Ed Sullivan introduced the new talent from Washington, DC named Sylvia Morrison. I sung Sam Cooke's song and danced to it as well.

By the time I left the stage, my ears were ringing. The entire audience was on their feet, standing with an ovation, Ma included. I peeped out of my peripheral vision and saw them. Seemed like bumble bees were everywhere! The buzz! The noise! The sound! Oh my God!

I saw Dewey Hughes off to the side smiling proud and happy. Helena and Vashti were jumping up and down hugging. I felt like I could fly! The people were applauding as if some big star had just closed the show. All I could think was "I didn't even do anything and they liked it like that? Thank you Lord!" Nothing I ever did or thought to do could compare with those few moments. It was the best feeling in my life. I couldn't stop smiling. The talent portion was over.

The general consensus was I would win the title of Ms. Congeniality. I got to thinking that if I won or placed as a runner-up, I would be the first contestant in this pageant to ever win in more than one category.

Unlike other pageants, Miss Black DC selected the fourth runner up out of the 15 leaving to the imagination that anyone's name could be next. Clint announced the 4th runner up. I didn't hear the syllables Sy__. I still had a shot. Next the 3rd and 2nd runner ups and there were still 12 girls to choose from. They still had not called Rasheeda.

They went through the whole thing about the first runner up's position, blah, blah, blah and should something happen to the winner, blah, blah, blah. Poochie must have thought they were calling the actual winner because right after that, Clint said "Sylvia Morrison." She jumped up on Howard's stage screaming "she won, she won" and realized at that point that they had just announced the first runner up. She almost died from embarrassment, but quietly came over to where I was and stood. She was so proud of me for being in the finals.

My heart was in the floor. Who could the winner be? None of the other girls proved themselves in the past to be a winner.

"And the winner is, Valerie Williams."

Valerie Williams? Who? What? Are they serious? No way. But wait a minute, she was magnificent. Nobody ever thought of her but she did and was by far the best.

I congratulated her for it even though I was depressed. I think we all were. We wanted to win, including Minnie Cohen. Her parents appeared on stage with their own trophy and quietly presented it to Minnie saying "you are our Miss Black D.C." I cried.

I went to find my mother and father but they were gone. Ma was sad I had not won. She didn't know how to display her emotions. Daddy was trying to get home to his drink.

The officials of the pageant whispered that they thought for sure I had the title in the bag. They felt Valerie would do well in the nationals. They told me to hang in there. Dewey fussed at me about the bathing suit competition and thought that was why I lost. Poochie said I should have won as everybody's family thought their girl should have won. Leonard showed up when it was all over. He forgot I told him to come.

I decided I wouldn't go back to Spelman but after losing I thought it best to return. I was afforded no opportunities as a result of being a runner up. No one called me for anything associated with the pageant, except Dewey. He still believed I had something going. We went in the studio to record a few songs. This allowed my first video, even though I, and most people, didn't know what a video was at the time.

It was campus news that I was first runner-up in the Ms. Black DC pageant. My buddies were patting me on the back saying "girl, you were almost there." I tried to figure out my next steps.

With a new roommate I was probably the only girl in the dorm on the weekends. Others were out on dates or doing something else. It was almost like girls gone wild because everybody was sleeping with everybody. I was too busy being loyal to Leonard, who for the most part forgot that I existed.

I grew tired of the bourgeois atmosphere at Spelman and decided to transfer to Howard University not knowing they were bourgeois too. I went through the rigorous application procedures and was accepted at Howard but unable to transfer any of my credits. No way could I do that because that would have been a year and a half wasted in school.

One of the girls from Spelman came by my room in a flight attendant uniform. She couldn't afford school at the time. She became a stewardess to save money to go back to school. Her family could fly for free and the benefits were good. The first thing that came to mind was I could go to Los Angeles, Hollywood, New York and continue to pursue my career if I became a stewardess too!

THE AIRLINES

As soon as I finished that semester, I went to Miami for an interview with Eastern Airlines and was hired. On December 29, 1972 an Eastern L1011 went down in the Florida Everglades. Most of the people died. They even made a movie about it. The crash worried Ma sick. She asked people to ask me not to go but I had already packed my bags and was on my way to Miami Beach.

That February we trained for 5 weeks. I was one of three Black girls in a class of about 20. Most of us were being based at LaGuardia and Kennedy Airports. My White roommate, whom I got along well with, suggested I stay with her in New York. The moment her parents saw me, said no way. She never told her parents I was Black.

Val, who is from Jamaica and a classmate from flight attendant school, was at the airport one day. We talked about our living arrangements. I told her I was staying in a hotel.

"I'm home with my parents. You should stay with us. My parents will not be afraid of you." She was right. They lived off the Grand Concourse at 174th St. in the Bronx. It was difficult and expensive getting from the Bronx to LaGuardia and/or Kennedy Airport. They were both far.

After weeks of trudging back and forth, I ran into another classmate from Miami. Charlotte was living with our personal appearance supervisor, Glenda Moss who had a house in the back of Kennedy Airport. Glenda was looking for another roommate and Charlotte was positive she would rent to me. She did. I thanked Val and her family for their hospitality and wished them well. I think of them often.

An attractive woman, Glenda was small and petite. She was light brown-skinned with lips that women today would die for, not too big and not too small. Her eyes were lazy but were often described by other flight attendants as sexy. They sort of closed when she smiled. Her face was round and her hair was short, brown and neat.

She had a no-nonsense kind spirit. If I had to think of someone she reminded me of today, I'd say either a young Chaka Khan or Mary J. Blige.

The airport was closer and the atmosphere was friendly. We talked about our pasts and hopes for our future. One night the whole household screamed at me because the trophy I had was so heavy I could hardly carry it. Glenda read the engraving. "FIRST RUNNER-UP - MISS BLACK NEW YORK."

I didn't want anyone to know that I was entering a pageant. The only thing I wanted to do was get a shot on television, be seen and meet people in the city. I would go to any lengths to get my foot in the door and the pageant would help get me do that and possibly to the finals for a shot on the nationals. I needed a state title to get there. Unfortunately, I didn't do it in New York.

The girls in the house figured I had to do well in order to be the first runner-up. I told them how Debbie Allen and her husband were there and how I tied for first place with Ber Nadette Stanis, who would later go on to become Thelma, JJ's sister in the hit sitcom, Good Times.

I was a little sad. I didn't win the state title and was not going to the finals. I would do almost anything to get to those finals, which is why I couldn't believe what happened next.

Charlotte asked if I would like to compete in the national competition for the Miss Black America title. I just looked at her. What? How could I compete after I had just placed in the New York competition? "Look, this is the entertainment industry. I want to be a star too."

A woman from her home town had the rights to 4 states. There was not enough Black population in Nebraska, N. Dakota, S. Dakota and New Mexico. She told me that if I was serious about being seen on a national level, this was my shot. I could represent one of those states.

I spoke with her and sure enough she said the pageant officials approved it. They knew that I had been in the New York pageant and said girls do it all the time. We agreed that I would represent the state of North Dakota and they would handle all press questions. She had no idea that I might shine.

When Glenda found out we were in the national competition she talked Eastern Airlines' executives into sponsoring us. This was getting serious.

THE NATIONALS

My first stop was to see Anna Wynn, Miss Black New York to let her know I was there. Her mouth fell open and her eyes got big.

"What are you doing here?"

"I'm a contestant representing the state of North Dakota."

After the initial shock, she laughed. "Girl, you are crazy! But I have to admit, I LOVE your drive and determination. You just won't give up!"

She had all kinds of questions which I somehow or another evaded but told her that I got clearance from the top. She grabbed and hugged me.

"I'm so happy to have you here but I have no plans on giving the title away. It belongs to me!"

Anna was tall, about 5'10", dark skinned and gorgeous. She sparkled like a piece of coal in the night. Her skin was flawless. Her face was almost the shape of a bowling ball with curves of art. Her nose was somewhat round and her lips were neither big nor small. She walked like a tiger, slowly gliding about with each long step making whoever was in her presence watch. She looked like she was straight out of Africa with the body of a queen. She was intelligent and able to communicate on almost any subject.

Whenever the judges asked her a question, she took a few moments to think about what was asked, raised her eyebrows, and answered like she studied the question. Anna was gifted with a talent beyond her years. She was awesome and I loved watching her in action.

As soon as she approached the stage, every one shut up because they knew royalty had taken its place. Anna commanded respect. She was in it to win and I knew it would take an awful lot to beat her. So far, I had not seen anyone anywhere that could touch her in the categories of talent, bathing suit or question and answer.

In the back of my mind, I didn't see how I was going to be able to beat Anna. Her talent consisted of reciting a poem written by the great James Weldon Johnson entitled "The Creation."

The first time I saw Anna perform, I thought God himself was creating the world all over again. Her long frame danced around in the most beautiful orange body fitting ensemble that flowed at the bottom allowing her feet and legs to do what they pleased. You could tell she was a professional dancer because with each move, she projected art. Her toes curved when she lifted her leg and that very leg, on the way down, took its time, making you watch the majesty of the flow embrace whoever was watching. You simply couldn't take your eyes off of her.

Her arms were sculpted like someone who lifted weights for years. There was not an ounce of fat on them. When she used the arms to express whatever she was talking about, you almost didn't hear her because they were spectacular. She held her head as if she was talking to her subjects. The neck was stiff and the head moved around on her neck like it was studying the world itself. The part in the poem where God "batted his eyes" was so awesome that I thought it was God really batting! I swear I had never seen anything or anyone like her.

My reason for being in the competition was for exposure to get on national television and get to Europe to entertain the troops. After that, anything could happen. I went ahead not realizing at the time how wrong it was. I was too excited and hopeful.

No one could beat Anna that year. Nobody. Had the competition been solely for talent, I may have walked away with it, but she was too beautiful, too smart and too grand. I picked a bad year to compete.

Anna won the title with me coming in as the 2nd Runner Up behind Miss Black Louisiana who thought she was cheated because she looked White. I was done with pageants. After the national competition, I returned to New York. Things were changing.

I was going out almost every night to the city seeking open mike clubs and places to perform. I don't know where I got the heart to tackle the streets of New York by myself every night alone and travel all the way back to Queens on public transportation, but I did. I never thought of being in any danger and was never afraid. I just wanted to perform, wherever. I had no girlfriends to hang out with and no men friends either. I was by myself but almost there, almost.

There was big talk of a layoff with the airlines of anybody with less than one year. I had 11 months and 3 weeks when I received my notification. They apologized for letting us go.

I hadn't heard from the Miss Black America contest. Maybe they didn't have a phone number for me.

I had no mentors, no one to turn to for any real guidance, or talk to about career choices, no managers, nobody. I was making decisions about career moves on my own not knowing what the outcome might be. I believe God sent a couple of his angels.

J. Morris Anderson, President and Owner of the Miss Black America Pageant lived in Philadelphia. I searched and found a number to call him. He was delighted to hear from me. They were trying to find me because I had been selected to go on tour. When could we talk? I almost had a fit. I was going to Europe.

THE MURDER

It was a cold day in January 1974. Right before they laid us off, I was heading to DC to see my family and friends and of course hoping to see Leonard. I took the first shuttle out of New York and arrived around 7:50 am. I hopped in a cab and stopped at Leonard's younger sister Regina's apartment. Regina's little 3 years old daughter was outside playing by herself in the courtyard. I found that mighty strange considering it was around 8 in the morning. I stopped, spoke and asked where her mother was.

"She's upstairs on the floor dead."

I looked at her concerned because that was really strange coming from a 3 year old. I repeated the question; she repeated the answer. I grabbed her hand and took her upstairs with me. I noticed the door to her apartment was ajar. I pushed it open and looked inside. On the right hand side, down the hallway, I saw her lying on the bathroom floor under the sink. Maybe she was drunk and had passed out? I walked toward her calling her name.

"Regina, Regina, girl get up."

No response. I was standing over her and noticed how strange she looked because she wasn't moving and it looked like she wasn't breathing. She was a little swollen but I assumed it was from drinking so much and probably being up all night.

The more I looked the more it occurred to me that she may be sick and need help. When I reached for her head to give her mouth to mouth resuscitation I knew something was seriously wrong. Her eyes were light gray. Regina had dark almost black eyes. There was also a gun laid next to her hand.

I ran out of the apartment grabbing her daughter who was in the hallway. I knocked on all of the doors. No one would open their door because most people had probably been up all night getting high or drunk or just not getting out of their bed to see who had the nerve to knock on the door that time of morning.

A neighbor heard me out in the hall asking if anyone knew Regina. She let me in to use the phone to call an ambulance once I told her what was going on. She headed to Regina's apartment. The next thing I knew, she was screaming,

"SHE'S DEAD, OH MY GOD, SHE'S DEAD, SHE'S DEAD, OH MY GOD!"

I never thought once until that moment that Regina could be dead. My mind started traveling. I never saw the bullet hole in her head until the police told me about it. Someone had shot her in the head, put a gun by her hand to make it look suicidal, left her for dead and then took her little girl outside and left her out there alone.

I wondered what time the murder occurred and what would have happened had I arrived at the time of the murder. Suppose I had knocked on the door seconds after it happened? Would the murderer have killed me too? Had her little girl saw or heard when they killed her mother? Was she right there, afraid, or know it was about to happen? How could someone come in and kill a 19 year old woman and leave her for dead like that, especially with a child present? The police took me down for questioning and got my statement.

It was not until Regina's ex-boyfriend was arrested in California for trying to kill another woman that they extradited him back to Washington and tried him for Regina's murder. He went to jail.

EUROPE

The girls selected to go to Europe had to be in Philadelphia for rehearsals at J. Morris Anderson's house in preparation for the tour. Jay was a character but strictly business. He showed no favoritism. I must admit that he really thought he was the cat's meow. He was tall, had a deep voice, thin and walked like he was bowlegged and pigeon toed. His afro was Black and full with matching eyebrows and mustache. He had long bushy sideburns and kind of reminded me of a pimp. He was handsome but it appeared that one of his eyes use to travel without the other one. He ignored you most of the time so thinking that you were cute and a bag of cherries meant nothing to him. His focus was the Miss Black America Pageant. Period.

The organization selected Miss Black DC, Esther, Miss Black Florida, Janice, Miss Black North Dakota, me and Anna, Miss Black America from New York.

I laughed at the other 3 girls when we got to his house because they talked about that man like a dog. Me too. We called the house the baby dungeon and couldn't understand how a house so grand could be so awful. It was a large, fabulous mini-mansion but the rooms were dark and needed painting. The lights must have been 10 watts and not one of the rooms had any color. I can't remember how many bedrooms there were but the furniture was old, the carpet needed cleaning, the dishes were just there -- some washed, some not. The whole house was basically dark.

I was shown to a bedroom that obviously needed a lot of cosmetic work. Furnished with old furniture, it looked, simply put, a mess. That room had probably not been painted in 200 years. The carpet was worn down to the padding. The window was shut and covered with an old piece of cloth preventing any light from outside trying to seep in.

As I prepared for bed, I got in what appeared to be already slept on sheets and closed my eyes real tight for fear of some unusual animal or bug appearing from out of nowhere. I must have made myself believe something was in the bed because I scratched myself for the longest time. I could smell a body odor in the comforter and the bottom sheet felt a little greasy in my mind. It probably wasn't but I was imagining all kinds of stuff. I finally fell asleep.

The attitude of Jay didn't change through all of that. He was a happy person, busting with excitement and treated us as well as he could. He had plenty of groceries but made us cook for each other. Nobody could cook, well, except me.

Jay wanted to put us up in a hotel, but according to sources, the organization had no money and after all, I thought it brave of him to open his home for us. Had reality television been out back then, we would have made for a grand television show.

We went over our parts, each person thinking or at least acting like they were the real Miss Black America. The time came for us to leave for our tour - first stop, Frankfurt, Germany.

I was 21 years old, leaving the United States of America for the first time, alone with 3 women I knew nothing about. I may not have won the title of Miss Black America, but I did what I set out to do. I appeared on national television and was going to Europe to entertain the troops of the United States of America. I was getting more exposure than I bargained for.

In Europe, we met a Lt. Colonel who was to be our chaperone and learned that we would get approximately $500 for the tour. They laid out the red carpet for us too. We had a limousine to take us to our destinations. I was pleased to be a part of this whole scene and thought about Corcoran Street and our coal and wood fire stove that kept the house warm. I thought about Ma who I knew was secretly proud of me. This was a far cry from those days. I closed my eyes and thanked God for the opportunity.

The first hotel we stayed in was absolutely gorgeous. I vaguely remember the red and orange colors in the lobby. Big, gigantic beautiful flowers everywhere! The doorman was handsomely dressed in a black uniform looking like he too was part of the American troops, perhaps an officer. The carpet was thick and the lobby was quiet. My eyes roamed and admired its splendor.

Unfortunately, the next day my world fell down. I was too sick from either food poisoning or the environment to get out of the bed. Charles Brown, a gentleman we met once we arrived in Europe, was actually in charge of the tour.

"Many people get sick their first time overseas. You might have to cancel the tour because you're too sick and we can't take a chance on you getting sick in every city. We'll see how you are in the morning."

I didn't like Charles at first. He seemed arrogant and big headed. I think that dark heavy thick beautiful beard and mustache must have given him the confidence of a king because he often threw his hand up as if to say "be gone!" He was short and stubby with piercing big, wide eyes. His nose was slightly pointed and his head was a little on the fat side. He had a gangster feel about him because he too was no-nonsense. He was neat and generally dressed for business in suits. Charles' looks put me in the mind of Rapper/Actor Ice Cube. He stammered but generally had something good to say and honest at the same time. "You're verr-ver-very tal-tal-talented but a lil-il-little too shy."

He was all about business and cared less about anything other than a smooth tour. He was also the manager of the group A Taste of Honey who eventually went on to win a Grammy for Boogie-Oogie-Oogie.

I woke up a little wheezy but didn't want to get sent home so I made myself have energy and proceeded to the venue for the sound check approximately one hour before the show. To our surprise, the place was packed with GIs. They gave us a really warm reception and I instantly felt better when we were about to take the stage. We each performed the act we did in the pageant. This was living.

Approximately 2 weeks into the tour, Esther was called home because of a tragedy in her family. Once she left, Janice was missing her boyfriend and wanted to go home. She got sick and left for Florida leaving me and Anna to carry the tour. Charles suggested we cancel but in less than one day, the two of us put together a show that would earn us standing ovations across Germany. We were pleased at how things turned out and decided once we got back to the states, we would continue with our show.

Countless newspaper articles, magazine stories, television interviews all proved that the two of us were awesome. Charles asked for my home phone number.

"I watched you almost the whole tour and told Redd Foxx about you. You need to prepare to go to Hollywood once you get back to the states. Man, Redd Foxx is going to love you!"

I wasn't sure if he meant it or not. Anna and I packed our bags, said goodbye to everyone, thanked them for their hospitality and headed back to the states. I took a lot of memories with me, especially our visit to the communist wall in East Germany that no longer exists.

I was glad to be back in Washington and happy to see my family. I couldn't wait to see Leonard who probably didn't even know I was gone and back. I called him. He invited me out that night to an after-hours spot where he casually introduced me to all of his friends in the underworld. I heard him telling people "yeah man, she just got back from Germany entertaining the troops. She's on me hard." I didn't even care that he said that because I was just happy to be in his company.

REDD FOXX

The very next day after I arrived in the states, I got that call from Charles Brown telling me that Redd Foxx was looking forward to meeting me. He asked if I could be ready to come to Los Angeles the next day. My heart skipped a beat. I couldn't wait. All of the arrangements would be made and there would be a limousine waiting.

I called Dewey to tell him my good news. He gave me some valuable information that day, something I continued to live with throughout my career.

"When you get to California they're gonna ask you to show them what you have. Don't hesitate Sylvia. Don't be shy, do not be afraid and do not waste their time. They have no time for foolishness and there is always someone waiting for those shoes to empty so they can fill them. It's a great opportunity and I'm proud. I know you will do well."

I landed in Los Angeles that afternoon, compliments of Redd Foxx. I didn't have time to check into a hotel or change clothes or anything because they wanted to see what they had heard so much about. My act was geared for large audiences and since there were only about 6 people in the room, I felt a little uncomfortable.

They all sat there in front of me waiting. Dewey was right. These people were serious but I didn't waste their time. I went right for the jugular. There was no applause, no audience reaction, only staring eyes. They were pleased that Charles Brown knew what he was talking about. That same day they had a contract for me to sign.

Like many young artists back in the day, I didn't have an agent, a lawyer or any kind of representative. The contract listed Redd Foxx's Company as my personal manager. They were asking for something like 35% in fees. I didn't know any better and didn't care. I was in California at the expense of Redd Foxx, the hottest man in television and was told how he would include me on some of the episodes of Sanford and Son. I signed the contract and was ready.

Today I think about how my kids would make it their business to call me to tell me when, how and if they were embarking on an opportunity like the one I had. I never called my parents and asked them for any answers. They knew I had a contract but as far as details, they never got involved because they just didn't know anything. It was okay, because I understood. I just wanted to do well and give them something in their life to be proud of.

I didn't get an assignment from the Redd Foxx organization nor did they help find a place for me to live but fortunately, I had a good friend living in L.A. who welcomed me to her apartment. I appreciate Joan Crowner. She was a designer and knew lots of people in L.A. Joan was funny, aggressive and a stranger to no one. She charged me no rent and basically let me stay there free for a whole month.

One night she took me to a friend of hers, whose husband was Wilbert Hart, an original member of the Delfonics. After casual entertainment conversation, he got his guitar out and had me sing an original song with him. I saw the look on Joan's face and knew that she didn't like the idea of someone stepping in her territory with her friends. When he asked for contact information she quickly made it clear that he could call her and she would make the connections. I never heard another word about him and when I asked her about him, she said she lost their information.

I went to an agency to find some temporary work as a legal secretary to earn extra cash until the real money started to flow. As much as I disliked working as a legal secretary, I had to make a way for me to eat.

I was going to different clubs, checking out the scenes and trying to get in on anything. One night, I talked my way in to a gig with the Temptations. They were giving them some type of local award. It was an all Black club and the people were partying hard. They introduced me and may as well have said go to the bar and get some drinks because nobody paid any attention to me. I called myself doing the act I did from the pageant and those people were no more interested in seeing me than a man in the moon. I heard someone in the audience say, "Oh give the girl a chance." I walked off stage and nobody could have cared less. They didn't even know I was there.

I went back to the apartment depressed. I could never go back on a stage and get that type of reaction. I had to insure that never happened again. I stayed in the apartment a whole week writing and working on material. That Ed Sullivan Show didn't work so I had to come up with something different. I knew the truth worked so I started there. The airlines! Who couldn't identify with that?

Ernestine, a character Lily Tomlin created would be an excellent flight attendant. She could make the announcements and then introduce Dionne Warwick, who would sing. Dionne could introduce her friend Diana Ross and she could introduce Cher and Nancy Wilson. The show would close with Sarah Vaughn and me telling people who I was. I worked on that set and worked on it until it was flawless. It was time for me to leave the apartment and try it out.

I went to a place on Sunset Boulevard called the Comedy Store where all of the big boys practiced new material. Unlike New York, Hollywood didn't have a user friendly public transportation system so I was on my own. My first night at the Comedy Store showed me just how serious this business was. The line for open mike was down the street and stretched forever. I signed up to perform and was something like number 19. They explained you had 5 minutes on stage and if they liked you, you would get asked to come back.

People in line were friendly and most of them had already been there before. I met people and thought for a minute that I might be in the wrong place because in actuality, I was not a comic. I was an entertainer, something like a Sammy Davis, Jr. I happen to do impressions which made people laugh and I also sang, which really was my number one talent as far as I was concerned. The ingenuity of the impressions is what impressed people the most so I focused on that. I never called myself a comedienne. It was the industry that labeled me that title.

I walked on stage pretending like I was confident. In less than 2 minutes, the room was applauding and laughing. They liked what they heard and saw. After that five minute routine, someone told me that the owner of the club - and I want to say her name was something like Mitzy - wanted to speak with me.

"Bunny, you were awesome. I'd like for you to visit our West Hollywood Store, put together a 20 minute set and once you're ready, come back here for a weekend spot."

At that time, I was going by Bunny Morrison. I couldn't wait to get back home to tell Joan. I was scheduled to be at the West Hollywood Store that coming Thursday.

The venue was totally different from the Sunset Boulevard Store. It was right off the beach and had a totally different feel. Since I was the newest kid on the block, I was last in line. By the time I got on stage, almost all of the audience was gone. I was a little sleepy myself and needless to say my performance was not all that because there was nobody there to perform to except for maybe 2 or 3 others. I went back to the comedy store after practicing my set and went out for drinks with a couple of guys, sodas to be specific for myself because I didn't drink. We talked about what we wanted to do with our careers.

"I want to host my own talk show."

The other guy although was funny had other dreams.

"I want to be an actor and do movies."

When asked what I wanted to do, I had it all planned out.

"I wanna do television specials every few weeks like the Sonny & Cher show. I'd like to invite the biggest names in the entertainment business and get a singer, actor or actress and a sports star on each show. Yep. That's what I wanna do."

"I believe you're going to do it too Bunny. Nobody is like you. You're different. You're the only female doing what you do. You'll probably be the biggest thing in the business."

I decided to look for a place and found a fabulous apartment around the corner from Joan. The rent was high but I needed my own space. It was already furnished so all I had to do was move in. I thanked Joan for her help and company hoping she liked my new apartment.

HOLLYWOOD AND SEX? FOR REAL?

I met Johnny Brown, also an impressionist, most remembered for his part as Bookman on the TV series Good Times. A happy round short outgoing personality, I liked him right away. He was funny and quick witted.

He invited me to a celebrity basketball game where the Jacksons were a team, but no Michael. On the way home we talked about what I needed to do to get situated in the entertainment industry. He asked could he come in. It was a little late but I figured what the heck. I was enjoying the conversation.

I fixed us a cup of tea and sat down on the couch beside him not even for one minute thinking anything other than we were there just talking. Before I knew it, he was rubbing my hair. My initial reaction made me remove his hand off of my head. His attitude was quiet and shocked.

"Sweetheart, you've got to learn the rules of this industry. You scratch my back and I'll scratch yours." I didn't know what that meant at the time.

"So what does that mean?"

He looked at me as if I was kidding. When he said that I'd have to do favors in order to get favors, I asked him to leave. I was way too old fashioned for that nonsense. It reminded me of the time Charles Brown asked if I'd be willing to have sex with a couple of company owners in exchange for stardom. When I said no, he said I had the wrong attitude.

"Oh, so you'll have sex with dudes for free and get nothing but you won't have sex with men for money and a whole new way of life? Somebody's been teaching you wrong young lady."

He was right and then dead wrong. What he failed to realize was I had scruples and I had to live with myself. I didn't graduate from get what you want through sex school. I never planned to attend it any way.

I continually called Redd Foxx, who was a busy man but I never really got a chance to sit down with him for any real length of time to talk. I was doing my own thing and realized that if I got a deal somewhere else, I wouldn't be able to take advantage of it because I was still under contract. It became difficult to speak with any one at the company to a point where I stopped calling. I was also getting homesick so I decided to move back home. It had been months.

I was happy to see Momma and Daddy and by this time Poochie had a son, who I nicknamed Scooby. This little guy gave my parents' house a whole new meaning. We all adored him.

My older siblings had kids too. Jerry's son was Andrew who we called Boo, we called Chubby's son, Stevie and Peter's son, John, III we called Bucky. Howard also had a son, Howard, Jr. They all were living with their parents at the time. Peter's daughter, Leslie, Bucky's sister could have been my daughter since she looks a lot like me. He ended up having a total of 8 kids. Poochie eventually gave birth to Cashana.

I got a phone call. A friend of Glenda's boyfriend, Bill had a friend who was in commercial advertisement and was promoting the 3rd Annual Rhythm & Blues Awards. He told her about me and assured her that I was the person she wanted to open the Awards show in Los Angeles. I was to meet with her the next day in New York.

I got the job. She said she knew I had to be good because he would never recommend anyone unless they were worth it. She booked me on a flight to Los Angeles, got a hotel room and explained that there was no money to pay me. They used my pay for my flight and hotel. I didn't care because I wanted to be in Los Angeles, especially since Patti LaBelle and Lawrence Hilton-Jacobs, from Welcome Back Kotter were hosting the awards.

The show started before I knew it. The audience was impressed after I performed and Bill's friend was satisfied.

I took notice of Patti LaBelle the whole while she was on stage. Her antics and movements were easy to copy. I could do an impression of her!

The Grammys were being held that night as well. I was already dressed. There was no way I could be in Los Angeles across from the Grammys and not go, especially since A Taste of Honey, Charles Brown's group was up for a Grammy for Best New Artist.

They won. At the after party, I sat at their table and I think everybody who was anybody was there. Lawrence Hilton Jacobs flirted the whole night even though he was with someone. Hollywood.

On the way back to the east coast, I thought about Patti. She was awesome, people loved her and I could talk and sing just like her.

DADDY 2

Daddy was sick and had been admitted to Veterans Hospital in Washington, DC being monitored because several parts of his body were not functioning properly. The ongoing drinking of alcohol and not eating properly was taking its toll. The surgery he had on his hand had also been a physical traumatic experience. Sometime around April 8, 1977, he went into a coma and was moved to the Intensive Care Unit.

I thought about how he originally hurt his hand. He was working on his car and the hood fell on it almost chopping the middle finger on his left hand off. He must have stayed in the hospital off and on for about 2 years. The doctors operated and moved his fingers around so that it would appear that he didn't have one missing. It was surgery I'd never heard of and Daddy was probably a guinea pig. I must admit, the hospital treated him well and I'm not sure how that surgery helped but he was written up in several articles about that procedure and how it was a medical breakthrough. I hoped that he would get well so that I could take him back to France to see the family he stayed with when he was serving in the Army.

Ma, who rarely visited anyone in the hospital, decided she'd better visit him this time. His pressure declined and he went downhill. They worked on him until there was nothing else they could do. He died on April 13, 1977. That was the first time I ever saw Ma cry. I started crying too and was going to miss him. I was his girl and now the one person I knew for sure loved me, was gone.

David Reavis, a guy I was seeing at the time heard about my father and came to see me. He was the one male friend Ma and Daddy kind of sort of liked a little teeny bit. He was there the whole while we prepared for Daddy's arrangements and stuck by me through the funeral.

We buried Daddy and I saw a change in Ma unlike anything I had seen in her before. She was quiet, humble and hurriedly got his business taken care of. She put him away like a king making sure he looked like a gentleman for his home going services. She dressed him in his best suit, a light blue single button jacket and made sure his white hair was brushed to perfection. I looked at Daddy in the casket and realized what a handsome man he was.

Because he was a veteran of 2 wars, I was looking forward to the 21 gun salute they give soldiers. He was proud of having been in the Army and hung pictures of himself in his uniform proudly.

On the day of his funeral, they folded the flag and presented it to Ma, but didn't give him a 21 gun salute. The United States of America robbed him of that honor. The soldiers left in order to give the 21 gun salute to an officer who was being buried that same day. The officer took seniority over Daddy. That was unacceptable to me.

I wrote to the President of the United States to find out why this happened and of course my letter got passed down, and passed, and passed until finally someone from the Department of the Army sent me a quick note apologizing, saying that I should write my Congressman. There was nothing they could do.

Since then, and in honor of my father, I write a letter to each new president telling him about the dishonor the United States of America did and probably thousands of other soldiers across the nation. Daddy was proud to have been an American solider and for all that he did, the least this country could have done was give him his rightfully deserved 21 gun salute that he proudly spoke of. To leave his gravesite and move on to an officer's grave was a slap in the face for me and my family and I have never gotten over it. Where ever he is, he knows that I didn't sit down on this one and will continue to fight for him until I die.

MA 2

I decided to stay on the east coast for Ma's sake because it seemed she was sad all the time. I asked her what it was she missed the most about Daddy.

"Every night before I went to bed, he would bring me a tall glass of ice water. Whether I drunk it or not, it was there, every night."

I told her I could bring her the water, but she said it was not the same. It was him. He was the only one that could do it. I decided to go back to New York. It was the first time in my life Ma gave me a stamp of approval. She reached under her mattress where she kept a little bankroll and handed it to me.

"Here. Take this."

I looked at the little roll of money. I couldn't move. She was giving me all of her money. I couldn't stop the tears.

"I can't take this Ma. You need this money."

"I believe that you're going to be somebody Bunny. It's in my heart."

I grabbed her and shocked myself. For the first time in my 24 years I hugged her. My chin and face side were buried in her shoulder and neck area. It was the first time I ever felt what it was like to hug my mother. More tears formed and my sniffles and shaking were becoming evident. I have no idea what she was thinking. It was the best hug I ever had. I left the room with a thickness in my throat. I was leaving for New York the next day.

I cried a lot when Daddy died because I missed him so. I also cried because I had never seen Ma so sad. I traveled back and forth from New York to see her maybe once a month and would see David too. He was hanging right in there with me.

Sometime in late August, 1977, Poochie called and said Ma had to go in the hospital for testing so of course I went home. Momma actually walked to the corner of where we lived and caught a cab to Sibley Hospital with basically nothing wrong with her, with the exception of a broken heart. She was suppose to come right back home that day, but apparently after running tests they decided to keep her for observation.

She was a sad person in the hospital. Rarely talking and openly depressed. You could tell she missed her husband. It was heart wrenching watching. Her eyes moved slowly and she never smiled. She stared in the air and didn't want to eat or drink. She was clearly heartbroken. Her spirit was deteriorating. It was easily visible.

On September 18, 1977, she was almost motionless. I left the hospital early that day. She died around 7:30 that evening. It was a quiet night. Still. Sad. Emotional. I didn't feel like talking to anyone, but I didn't want to be by myself either. An eerie feeling took over me and I was immediately going into depression. Was this a dream? No way could Ma be dead. Daddy just died! It's not true! NO.

Quite frankly I didn't know what to do with myself. I was already grieving for Daddy who had only died 5 months before. Now when I cried, I didn't know who I was crying for.

We made arrangements and buried Ma. My family asked me to sing at her funeral and I looked at them like they were crazy. Who sings at their own mother's funeral? They all said that she would love it if I did that. I thought about it real hard and decided to do the James Cleveland version of Jesus Is the Best Thing. I got through it. I must say I love Poochie. Even in the midst of something as devastating as our mother dying, she and I sat together and cried together. She pointed out the faces of a few people at the funeral who looked like cartoon characters crying. We both laughed at their faces so hard we had to hold our eyes. People thought we were hysterically crying about Ma's death but we were in stitches laughing at the different characters we saw. We talk about those moments to this day.

Once the services were over, I had to figure out what I was going to do. We weren't going to keep the house because my sisters and brothers were either married, had children or both. I was the only single child of my parents with no children. Ma had a small estate. It was not a huge estate but enough for me to buy a car she wanted me to have. I got the car, a red 1978 Ford Granada, 4 doors with leather seats and went straight to David's house to show him my new ride.

THE CAR

David was a 6'6" handsome man, with dark features. He had black hair, a black moustache, dark handsome eyes that appeared to grab you. The color of a baseball bat, he was a big guy but in tip top shape with perfect proportions for his height. He looked like he could have been a statute when he stood still. He smiled like a king. I use to see the ladies staring at him when we were out. He was friendly and most times had something fresh to say to the females. I tried to act like I didn't care because sometimes you just have to do that.

He liked the car and so did I. I had only been from the dealers a couple of hours when I invited him to take a ride in it, not noticing the orange he had in his hand. He started peeling the orange wasting juice all over the seats and the carpet in my brand new 3 hour old car. Juice was spitting a little on the dashboard, the passenger window and he was shaking the juice off his hand.

"David, please don't eat the orange in here, okay?"

He looked at me disgusted as if I had highly insulted him. We were both quiet after I said that and I continued to drive. I tried to make conversation but he was quiet.

"Pull in the driveway over there behind Spingarn."

Spingarn High School is in a hood section of Washington, and its driveway is secluded, away from the public's eye. I did.

"Pull up behind the building. I have to take a leak." I did.

We sat there for a moment, David looking straight ahead. I was wondering why he didn't get out of the car to use the bathroom. He just sat there. I was looking around at the scenery.

From out of nowhere, totally unexpected, he took the orange and rammed it in my face, causing my nose to spurt blood all over the front seats, the window and my new coat. I saw stars of all colors!

"You have a lot of nerve not wanting me to eat in this car."

I was trying to get the stars out of my eyes because the hit was so devastating I almost couldn't breathe. I wasn't sure if my nose was broken or what. Before I could get myself together he opened the driver's door, undid my seatbelt and pushed me out of my own car onto the ground, bloody face, bloody coat, bloody hands and all. He drove off in my brand new car and left me in the back of the school with no purse, no money, and no nothing.

I couldn't move, nor make sense of what just happened. I was in a daze. Was this a dream? Why did he do that? It felt like needles in my nose and blood was everywhere! I cried for about 5 minutes, making it sting more. My head hurt and so did my heart. I kept softly touching my nose to make sure it was still there. IT HURT SO BAD! I had nothing to wipe away the blood!

I was still sitting on the ground when I heard the car coming back. He opened the passenger door and told me to get in. I didn't want to argue with him, but I promised myself if I ever got out of this madness, he would never have to worry about me again.

He actually grabbed and hugged me saying he was sorry. I kept trying to figure out how I missed this part of his personality? Where in the world was it hiding because I never, ever saw any remnants of it? "You were treating me like I was nobody just because you have a new car."

I went along with everything he said until I could get that mad man out of my car. Nobody would ever, ever hit me like that and expect to maintain a relationship with me. We pulled up to where he was staying.

"Call me later on." I casually said ok and rode out of his life.

In late 1977 I moved back to New York in hopes of continuing to pursue my career. I thought of my parents all the time. The grief was unbearable. Every time I started crying for one, the other one came in the picture. I think I lost my mind. For real.

It was difficult traveling from Glenda's house to the city especially since I was trying to do a lot of open mike clubs at night.

I spoke to Mertine Moore, Rasheeda's sister, who was also modeling with the Wilhelmina Agency in New York. She told me that Shebah Aqeel, another model from Washington, DC, was looking for a roommate and suggested I give her a call. Shebah rented the apartment from Rasheeda who rented it from Iman, the supermodel.

I called Shebah, went to see her and we hit it right off. I moved in that week after bidding my goodbyes to Glenda and vowed to keep in touch because she had been so good to me. I hugged her tight and had tears in my eyes because Glenda was one of the most giving, free hearted, free spirited people I knew. I promised myself that if I ever became famous, I'd find her and do something that would show partly how much I appreciated her. It was on to New York City.

SHEBAH

I walked in Shebah's small, tiny apartment stepping directly in the kitchen as soon as you entered. There was a small refrigerator that was about as tall as my knees, a small stove, like a child's Easy Bake Oven and one little counter with a couple of cabinets. It was the smallest kitchen I ever saw, almost like a doll baby's kitchen. The living room was small as well. It seemed like after about 5 steps you were through the living room to the bedroom.

This baby apartment was located at 78th and 3rd Avenue in the heart of the East Side of New York City. There was a doorman and the personality of the building was quiet but wealthy. People came back and forth gently yet with a sense of urgency. The little dogs were everywhere and the doorman was usually at attention, even when the shifts changed. Any request you asked the doorman followed with expecting a tip. Of course I didn't know that at the time and asked for favors every chance I got. "Can you give Shebah this package when she comes in?" or "When the mailman gets here can you accept my package?" No wonder he looked at me all crazy when I walked away! Of course Ms. Shebah straightened me out right quick. "Don't forget to tip the doorman." That got old right quick. I started doing my own favors.

Shebah and I were perfect roommates, so different yet so alike. She was a high fashion model and spent a lot of money to look good from her hair right down to the 4 inch heels she wore day and night. About 5'10 inches tall, she could have weighed no more than 115 pounds. Her thin frame was curvy and everything about her matched. Her skin was smooth and put you in the mind of light brown sand on a beach. Any make up applied did itself a favor because Shebah's beauty really needed no makeup. Her eyes were bright and the face! That face! Rosey red cheeks and pure red lipstick applied to her small lips made her skin color stand out. The dark makeup surrounding her eyes drew you to her making you want to stare and see how the makeup was applied. Her neck was long and she took her time looking around. You could almost watch the clock while she turned her head. She took her time in everything she did. The girl was gorgeous.

She believed in the best. She was in full control of just about everything she did. When she sat down it was as if she was in front of a camera. Her long, smooth, shiny legs stood out. Her feet were manicured as were her hands. She had boyfriends galore and chose which ones she would see and when. They all adored her and showered her with gifts, if she accepted them. Only diamonds for her. Almost every man she met was in awe of her beauty.

I often think how spectacular her lounging clothes were. When I first arrived at her apartment she had on pink silk pants and a silk pink button up blouse, a flowing Diana Ross robe and pink high heeled bedroom slippers with fuzz all around the middle part of the slipper. She walked like a tiger and shined with confidence. I wondered if she'd be able to put up with my silliness. If I put on bedroom slippers with heels, I'm going to fall down. The old adage "opposites attract" fit us perfectly.

She told me that a friend of hers planned lunch and she was taking me. Her friend was obviously wealthy. We stopped by his richly decorated law firm where he was in conference with one of his clients. When introductions were made, I swear I had seen the client before. He was a white guy with a beard and really nice round eyes. The attitude in his face was a sad one. His voice sounded familiar but where would I have known him from? We shook hands with the client and he left. "He looks awfully familiar." Shebah looked and said, with her sexy voice, "Why of course. That was Paul McCartney." I wanted to slap both of them.

We had to wait a little longer than we planned and the attorney couldn't go to lunch with us. He offered Shebah his unlimited American Express card and told us to go shopping on 5th Avenue. You should have seen me looking like a kid in a candy store. Shebah politely refused the card and said she had something to do after lunch and thank you but no thank you. I was making all kinds of scrunch faces trying to motion her to get the dag gone card, but Ms. Class declined.

Another time, an attorney that Shebah was dating and a member of the National Negro Golf Association suggested to the group that they bring me to their annual meeting being held in the Poconos as the entertainment for their event.

Of course they immediately obliged considering Shebah made the suggestion. She introduced me to the attorney's friend who happened to be a dentist. I already knew I was way too silly for this serious group of professional African American lawyers, doctors, dentists, judges and so forth, so there was no need in me trying to develop a relationship with or impress this guy. To my surprise, he actually thought I was all that and a bag of chips, especially when I performed that night to Donna Summer's "Hot Stuff."

I came out on that song with a somewhat revealing outfit. It was a 2 piece with a tight top exposing my midriff and a Brazilian skirt made in layers spreading out from the waist to the knees. Whenever you moved in that skirt the whole room moved with you. Not a person on this earth could tell me that night that I wasn't hot. The top was so tight that the minute I walked out on the stage it burst causing almost all of my goodies to be exposed. I was fortunately, able to conceal it immediately. It stopped the show and I had to regroup, but all of the guys thought it was part of the act and howled when it happened. I on the other hand, almost had a stroke considering I was only about 100 pounds and no chest whatsoever. They must have talked about that event for a long time, wives included.

I was trying to work all of the open mike night clubs including Rodney Dangerfield's. Every time I'd go there, the hosts said they already had a full lineup or just kept me waiting.

"Think I can get a few minutes this week?"

The host took a deep breath like I was on his last nerve. He rolled his eyes in the air and then, all of a sudden, he came up with a bright idea! I would go on behind some dude who, according to his snicker, was a beast on stage. He laughed and said something like "I don't know if you wanna go up behind this dude. When he's done, there may not be a room."

He was right. When the comic got off stage, there was nothing left but smoke from his heels. He murdered the room and drained the audience of almost every laugh they could muster. They were still mumbling after the performance. The host could have cared less. He got on stage, bragged about how awesome Jay Leno, a struggling comedian, was and immediately introduced me. (Yes, Jay Leno.)

"We have a young lady about to come out here and do a little impression for you. Somebody said she does LilyTomlin. You do LilyTomlin right? Please welcome Sylvia Traymore."

That was it? That was my introduction? About to come out and do a little impression? I was accustomed to this. Most of the rooms didn't want me in there anyway. They never had a spot or any time for me and when they did it was 3 minutes on stage. Period. My heart dropped. But I finally got some time and I wasn't going to lose it.

I laughed to myself. I spoke into the microphone and didn't expect to get any attention. But wait. They shut up. They were listening. Oh my God! They were paying attention! I did my set and although it was nothing like the energy that Jay Leno displayed, they actually enjoyed it and did so with a miniature standing ovation!

Now I don't know if that was a result of riding off the crest of Jay's performance, but it happened! I was allowed to go to the Dangerfield club and get on almost whenever I wanted after that.

I also worked other clubs including the Improv and local clubs that often showcased people like Jerry Seinfeld. He gave me advice on a portion of my act to make it more effective. I, in turn, told him what I thought he could do in a part of his act. He just looked at me! We both laughed. Who had any idea he was going to be as big as he became? In the 1970's he was nobody just like most of us.

It was a similar experience when I met Rosie O'Donnell. She was doing her version of the Wizard of Oz and her set was only about 15 minutes. It was awesome. She told me she loved my Dionne Warwick. I didn't know she knew who Dionne was.

It took a while to develop the relationship I had at a lot of the clubs. Many nights, clubs that hosted open mics would not give me any time. I can't tell you how many nights I walked the streets alone, unafraid looking for a microphone to try out or redo my material. I never saw any other Black females in New York at that time doing comedy.

There were nights when I wanted to sign on but I was told there's no more time, or there were too many people or they just couldn't. What bothered me is that nights when the White guys came in after me and wanted time, they got it. Now, maybe they called ahead of time or maybe they were regulars, I don't know. I do know that I thought it mighty strange that they were given time.

The only way I got time is if patrons asked if I was performing. I dealt with it and made the best of the time I was allowed.

I ran into Billy Crystal's manager and talked him into coming to see me at an open mic. I did a set with a band I met that night. We were a complete mess and I was not impressive at all. I looked up and he was gone. I was heart sick. I would never, from that moment on, try to impress someone with something I'd never done on stage before.

I wanted to sell my idea of a television special to one of the major networks. It would consist of a major song artist, an actor, a sports figure and me. I knew I could do it and was going to do it. Sammy Davis, Jr. was coming to town at the Waldorf Astoria. I definitely wanted Mr. Davis on the show.

Shebah and I were sitting in the apartment when I saw the advertisement in the paper. He was going to be a guest at a Jewish dinner. The tickets were $1,000 per person. I had to speak with Mr. Davis. Not only could I solicit him for my TV special, he knew Johnny Carson and to get on the Carson show would send your career skyrocketing.

"You have lost your mind. No way are you even going to get in the building." Shebah thought I'd lost my mind.

"I have nothing to lose."

I started getting dressed. She saw how serious I was.

"I'm going with you."

For some reason she believed me and wanted to see. She got dressed and looked like a movie star.

On the way to the Waldorf, I heard an advertisement that Muhammad Ali was being roasted at the Apollo Theatre. Muhammad Ali, the most popular man in the world was going to be right there in the city and NBC was taping it. I had to get on that show and I knew just how I was going to do it. I would dress up like a Black Ruth Bussey, a huge star from the hit show Laugh In and crash the stage with my impression of her.

We went straight to the Waldorf Astoria's Penthouse where the dinner was taking place. Shebah and I looked mighty strange sitting there in the lobby because we were not just the only 2 Black women we were the only Black people period. We had been sitting for a while and no Sammy. An hour or so later, no Sammy. She said we should leave because she didn't think Sammy was coming. As she was voicing her thoughts, a crowd came through and to our surprise Elizabeth Taylor got the elevator off with her entourage. It was the first time I had ever seen Ms. Taylor up close. She was beautiful and courteous. She spoke to everybody and I was proud to be there in her presence. Some of her entourage looked at us as if to say who the @#% are they?

About another hour later, Shebah was convinced that Sammy was not coming. She had me almost convinced too but I hung in there until there was almost no one out in the hall. The program was about to start and Shebah insisted we leave. We got on the elevator heading back to the lobby when I noticed way down the hall, a little black spot coming up the corridor. The spot was short and had a few other black spots with it. It was him!

I grabbed Shebah's arm and hopped back on the elevator to the penthouse floor. I wanted us to already be there when he got off the elevator. Once we got back upstairs, my heart started beating because I knew at any moment he would be getting off that elevator. "What are you going to say to him? You don't stand a chance in hell of getting close to him."

Everything she said was negative and I don't believe she meant it to be that way.

The elevator doors opened and there he was. Sammy Davis, Jr. He stopped, looked around, saw us and said "Good evening ladies." We both said good evening. He headed for the sign in table. "What are you going to do now? You just let him slip through your hands and said nothing."

By that time, the Davis entourage was going into the dining hall. We missed our shot. I sat there trying to figure out what to do next when a big Black guy walked up to us and introduced himself to us. His name was Don.

"Hello ladies. What brings you here?"

Shebah and I were on two different wave lengths. I didn't want him to know that we secretly came there to see Sammy so I said we were waiting on our dates. At the same time I said that, Shebah said we were there to meet Sammy. He looked at both of us a little confused.

"So what do you do?"

Shebah, in her sexiest voice said "I'm a model/singer." and I told him I was a comedienne/singer/entertainer, much like Mr. Davis.

"Where are you working?"

Again, Shebah and I were on two different waves. Her attitude was if you are anybody, you should be able to help me. My attitude was if I'm any good I should be working somewhere. She said she was working nowhere, I said I was working at Dangerfield's, forgetting that Mr. Davis and Mr. Dangerfield were friends. It was true I was working at Dangerfield's but I was only working the open mike night. This was not open mike night.

Don was delighted because he said that they were looking for something to do that evening and going to Dangerfield's was a good idea.

"I'll bring Sammy by."

Our eyes almost popped out of our heads. I had to get over to Dangerfield's and ask could I perform! I went back to the apartment, changed clothes and headed straight to Dangerfield's. There was no open mike that night but my good friend David Copperfield was hosting the show. Although he had the same name as the magician they were clearly not the same person.

I asked David if he could let me do about 10 or 15 minutes. He looked at me like I was crazy. Tonight, Rodney was performing and no one else was scheduled to be on the bill. I told him the Sammy Davis, Jr. story. He thought about it for a moment and looked me in my eye.

"Sylvia, you can go on for 10 minutes and 10 minutes only. You can't do more than that. I'm laying my career on the line for this."

I grabbed and hugged him and told him he would not be disappointed. At 10:00 pm I didn't see Don or Sammy come in the door. It was time to go on stage. Shebah and Rasheeda were both there but no Sammy. David introduced me as a surprise guest and I went on - still no Sammy. I went through my routine and the audience loved it - still no Sammy. As I was thanking the audience for allowing me their time, in they walk, several of the entourage. The only thing they saw or heard was the applause from the audience and me walking off the stage.

Just my luck they didn't see me. I went to the table where Mr. Davis was and Don introduced us. The first question Mr. Davis asked had my heart racing.

"Was that applause for you?"

"Yes! It sure was."

"Send me a tape, okay?"

"I sure will. Thank you!"

He turned around focusing his attention elsewhere. I wanted to go back on that stage so bad but I knew that David Copperfield couldn't let me because Rodney was ready. Again, I was almost there, almost.

This was at least an opening for me to contact him for my television special. I believed I had that one locked down.

The sports figure I was interested in was Julius Irving - Dr. J. They called him Dr. J because he operated on the court - at least that's what Raymond, my next door neighbor from uptown, told me. He said if I was going to use a sports figure, use Dr. J. He was the man. I had never heard of him but if Raymond said it, that was who I should get. Raymond knew his sports. I started seeing him everywhere, commercials, television, talk shows and radio shows.

I spoke to Raymond about getting someone who was not as popular as Irving. Julius was doing everything. Raymond suggested I check out Larry Kenon with the San Antonio Spurs. He was the hottest forward in the NBA and people would like to hear about him because he was starting to break records. That worked because the Spurs were coming to New York in a couple of weeks.

LARRY

I was scheduled to do a picture/head shoot with Rasheeda because she wanted me to have professional pictures for my performances. She was tired of me looking "generic." She was a top flight Wilhelmina model, been on the cover of many magazines several times, walked the runway for great designers and was simply awesome. I will never forget how she, a woman with all kinds of modeling experience, took me by the hand and led me around New York City like I was her personal project, and in actuality, I was. She never asked anything of me other than to pay attention and follow her lead. It was my first "Tyra Banks" experience. We were all over NY getting hair done, make up applied, trying on clothes, etc. She just liked me and I appreciated her doing that. I told her she had an open invitation to all of my shows.

The makeover was transforming. I kept looking at myself in the mirror because I didn't even look like the same person! My hair was cut short in layers, a little of it swaying over my eye for a sexy effect.

The dark red almost burgundy cheek rouge was bold but pleasant. They placed hints of red tone colors on both sides of my chin and added the same color in sections of my forehead. There were highlights that went under my eyes to hide my dark circles. I was fortunate to have smooth skin because when they powdered my face my skin looked flawless.

The eye makeup artists kept saying "look up please" or "hold your head a little low but look to your left." I jumped every time they tried to apply the pencil to the lower part of my eye but the Gay makeup artist in charge came over and said "Boo Boo, it's okay daw-ling! You'll be just fine Boo Boo. Just sit still and watch the magic. Okay?' He/she snapped their fingers and the artists went to work. No way could I walk around every day with that much make up on. Shucks, when I took it off, people wouldn't know who I was!

She dressed me in an off the shoulder top where you could actually see my bones. Of course I only weighed about 110 pounds at that particular time but that was popular and in actuality, since I was only 5'6 ½ inches tall, that was considered a little on the heavy side.

My neck looked long and thin and I personally liked my lips. All my life they were like my mother's, so small and thin that unless I smiled you couldn't see them. They painted them so that you could see lusciousness in them. You couldn't tell me that I wasn't sexy! LOL! Rasheeda took a step back, looked at me real good, moved a piece of my hair off my face and smiled. "Girl, you look good!"

She had me looking like a real high fashioned model. I was so honored and thankful for her assistance. I never forgot that day because I learned how giving she was.

I would have never dreamed that years later she would be the woman associated with the Marion Barry scandal. I wish people knew the Rasheeda that I know. She's a beautiful person. That was an unfortunate incident and time in her and her family's life. I guess it was unfortunate for him too. I wish and hope the best for them.

The Spurs arrived in New York approximately 3 days after my photo shoot/makeover. I called the Spurs office to find out where they were staying. When I spoke to Larry Kenon I explained what I was doing. He sounded interested and was eager for a meeting. I was to meet him at the hotel. I had only seen him once and hoped that I was going to see the right person. I didn't want the homecoming experience to repeat itself with the wrong person showing up!

I knocked on the hotel room door. When the door opened I instantly came to life. He was tall, around 6'9" and almost bent over a little. His smile warmed my heart right off the jump. His afro was short, but neat. His eyes were mean, but kind at the same time. I guess the meanness came from the seriousness in the permanent frown that spent itself in his forehead. He seemed to be frowning even when he smiled.

You could easily feel his business sense. I couldn't help but notice that his nose reminded me of an Indian's. It was a rather large nose almost bent if you saw his profile. Hints of red tones danced in his skin. His lips, to me, were kissable. I loved how groomed his face looked. He was a darker brown than me and could have had a bad boy disposition. When he looked at you he almost stared.

He was obviously in shape and to me it looked like he worked out every day. I couldn't help but notice how large his hands were. His legs appeared almost bow-legged. His teeth looked perfectly straight as if he wore braces. They were shiny white. His comfortable mood put me at ease. He was simply put, in my eyes, one of the most handsome men I'd ever seen. I fell for him right away. It was at that moment I knew what love at first sight meant. There's not one man I can think of that puts me in the mind of him. He was in a lane all by himself.

I was glad that my hair still looked nice and I learned a few tricks from the makeup artist Rasheeda introduced me to. I wore a business suit hoping I was professionally impressive in what I was trying to pitch.

I tried not to show that I liked him because I was there on business. I was almost nervous. He asked me to give him a few minutes. Not a problem. He jumped in the shower, came back and apologized for taking so long and sat down with me while I went over my plans.

"I want to submit a proposal to one of the major television networks for a possible variety special." I proceeded. He was impressed with the idea that I did impressions.

"Do somebody."

I wasn't afraid but right then was not the time.

"You'll have to wait for our rehearsals."

The whole while we talked, he interrupted my conversation telling me how beautiful my eyes were, and how he liked my lips, blah, blah, blah. Quite honestly, I was falling for it.

We'd been talking for about a half hour or so when someone knocked on the door. Several people came in his room.

"I have to excuse myself but are you busy this evening? Maybe we could have dinner tonight.

I tried to act like I was busy but I already knew I would love to have dinner with him. I gave him the number and bid my goodbye.

"I'll see you later."

He kissed me on my cheek and I almost died. I was whisked away by his charm.

The minute I walked in the door, I told Shebah about my afternoon. She asked where I met him because she knew I had not been dating anyone. I explained the whole story to her.

"I'm in love." Shebah smiled.

A little later that evening, I left out to run to the store across the street and by the time I got back Shebah was gone. I didn't know she was leaving because I would have never left out for fear of missing the call. Remember, we didn't have Caller ID back then. I paced the floor because it was getting late. Did he call while I was out and I missed the call? Did he not call at all? Did he forget about me that quickly? Oh no. It was getting late, so I decided to call him.

He answered the phone, kind of like he was sleepy but perked up the moment he heard my voice.

"Did you call? I left out and wasn't sure."

He hadn't called and my heart dropped. I felt awful. He forgot about me that quickly.

"Hey, can you hop in a cab and meet me here at the hotel? We can grab something to eat."

My heart started fluttering again.

We walked around Manhattan, stopped and got a sandwich and talked and talked and talked until around midnight. He asked me to come up for a minute or two because he wanted to get my information in order to send for me to come to San Antonio. I obliged. We talked and laughed and talked and laughed until it got really late. I started yawning.

"Well, it's about that time for me to be on my way back."

"I really don't want you traveling alone late at night. You're welcome to stay here tonight."

Yeah right. There he was with one king sized bed and wanted me to stay in his room. Who or what did he think I was? I declined. He saw the look on my face and knew what I was thinking.

"If you think for one minute that I want to have sex with you, you need to think that over twice. I'm an NBA player and can have women whenever I want."

He assured me that I could stay and he would not touch me. He drew a line on the bed and said one side was his and the other mine. I believed him.

The next morning, I had never seen anything like the breakfast he ordered from room service. It was a spread fit for a queen. Everything was laid out from eggs to turkey, to bacon, to grits, to biscuits to muffins, oatmeal, fruit, coffee, tea, water, honey, waffles, pancakes, whatever. I couldn't believe my eyes!

He told me he was expecting company but didn't want me to leave. Burt Padell, an agent for some of the largest professionals and entertainers in the world, was coming to talk to him about representation. He wanted me to stay because perhaps Burt could help me as well. I thought that was pretty generous because he had never seen what I did.

I showered, got dressed and was happy my hair had not frizzed. Mr. Padell, a rather short gentleman was tall in confidence and all about business. Larry introduced us and I noticed that he was a little perturbed that I was there. He wanted to talk to Larry by himself.

"She's cool man. I ain't talking if she has to leave. She stays."

He outlined for him everything he could and would do as Larry's manager and finalized his conversation by giving him a couple of his cards. I guess to stay on Larry's good side he gave me a card too and told me to call him. He left.

The Spurs were playing the Knicks that night and Larry insisted I come to the game.

"Go home, get some clothes and come back to the room. And hurry, I don't want you gone too long."

I left on a cloud. I told Shebah all about how I loved every single minute with him. I went back to the hotel a little ashamed that everything that took place the night before was completely out of character for me. Thank God he didn't treat me like a one night stand.

He left a ticket in my name at the box office and I was to sit with his good friend whose name was also Larry. Prior to leaving for the game, he handed me an aluminum foil package and told me to give it to his friend.

"Don't open it but make sure Larry gets it. You'll know who Larry is because he'll introduce himself to you. After the game, meet me at Clyde's right outside of Madison Square Garden."

I followed all of his instructions and couldn't help but wonder what was in that aluminum foil. I didn't want to lose his trust by opening it after he told me not to, so when I got to Madison Square Garden, Larry, the friend, introduced himself to me. I gave him the aluminum foil pack. He smiled and said thank you. He was supposed to meet Larry after the game as well. At that time, I must have been one of the most naïve people in the world.

When the game was over Larry the friend and I went to Clyde's. It was packed. I saw Larry Kenon come in the door and my heart skipped a beat. He came straight to the table where I was sitting, reached over and gave me the biggest kiss on the lips.

"How did you like the game? You give Larry what I asked?"

We sat there for a while, ate some food and headed back to the hotel. Larry was leaving in the morning.

"I want you to come to San Antonio and spend some time with me."

At that point, I believed he liked me as much as I liked him, or at least he was acting like it. We hung out for a while and headed back to the hotel. That next morning, he told me to sleep as long as I wanted and check out of the hotel when I felt like it. He also wanted me to wait on his call in the next few days because he would be sending for me. Once he left, I felt like I died and went to heaven and couldn't wait to visit him in Texas.

In the meantime, Muhammad Ali was coming to town to be roasted. I was putting together my strategy to get on that roast and so far things looked good. Richard Pryor, the hottest comedian in the country, was hosting the event and the list of roasters went on forever. Some of the biggest names in show business were going to be there, which meant I had to be there too.

Larry called and told me there was a ticket at the airport. I was going to San Antonio, Texas!

He picked me up from the airport in an old Lincoln and we didn't talk that much in the car because the windows were down and my hair was flying all over the place making me look like a wild woman. I wanted so bad to ask to put the window up but it was hot outside and there was no air in the Lincoln.

He helped with my bags and got me settled in his beautiful house. It appeared that everything was built for his 6'9" frame. We went to the grocery store because he wanted me to have whatever I wanted at my fingertips to eat or cook even though we went to dinner that evening. We talked about any and everything making him more charming than ever. I couldn't help but wonder if he thought I was charming too because he looked in my eyes almost the whole while. I'm so silly. I kept trying to make my eyes dreamy. I probably looked like some kind of duck or something. It got late and we went to bed.

The next morning, his housekeeper was already straightening up his house. The golf equipment was ready.

"You know how to play golf?"

I almost burst out laughing because I had never been on a golf course in my life. Plus, I only packed high heels. He said he'd teach me.

The golf course was beautiful and so was the weather - the perfect day for golf. He taught me the basics but laughed every time I tried to move with those high heels on. My hair was flying everywhere and I looked a mess. Whenever the wind moves, my hair moves with it.

Once back to the house, we ate and Larry drove to the mall, stopped me in my tracks and said "I want you to buy whatever you want. Ok? Doesn't matter what you want - just get it." I didn't know what to get. I couldn't make up my mind but he told me he knew exactly what I needed. We went to the sports section and got sweat suits, tennis shoes, socks, and anything associated with sports. I loved everything he picked out for me. Now I could play golf for real.

We went back to his house and talked about the future.

"So what are you planning to do after basketball?" He had no immediate plans. "I think you will make a great sportscaster."

I quickly wrote a script for him. I sat there and watched him read the script and showed him several ways to deliver his words. He sounded good too. He loved it and had never done anything like that and liked that I was bringing that out of him.

"That's why I want to do a special because I love the entertainment business and love watching performances come to life. Besides, that's all I really know."

I only stayed a couple of days because I had to get home for some of the shows I was doing. A couple of weeks later he sent for me again. It was back down to San Antonio. We played more golf, ate out and enjoyed each other's company. The phone rang and I couldn't figure out how it was for me.

It was a call from Anna Wynn who said she got the number from Shebah. I gave Shebah the number right before I left in case of an emergency. Anna asked me to sit down because it was a big one.

"Richard Pryor declined hosting the Ali Roast. Dick Gregory was asked to do it but he declined as well. How about I was able to talk Dick Gregory and the producers into letting you host the Roast? Can you believe that?"

WHAT! Was she kidding? That was wonderful! All of the plans I had to crash the roast were now irrelevant. What a break and a blessing. I was actually going to host the Muhammad Ali Roast at the legendary Apollo Theatre in New York City. I had to leave right away.

Larry was not only happy for me, but wanted to go too but had a game out of town that next day. The limousine was going to be at the airport waiting for me. My career was really picking up but I missed him the minute I got on the plane.

THE ROAST

It was April 13, 1979. The limousine was right there when I arrived. While driving to the Apollo, I must have smiled the entire time. I was never more excited in my life. At the Apollo I was basically told to do what I needed to do to host it. There was no script. I guess since they initially expected Richard Pryor, Frankie Crocker or Dick Gregory, they felt no need for a script. This was my thinking. I interviewed each of the roasters individually in order to try to figure out how to introduce them and what I would say. First stop was interviewing football player Jim Brown, then Fred Williamson, Pele, Dick Cavett, Harry Belafonte, Donna Summer, LaWanda Page, Whitman Mayo, Garrett Morris and the other roasters to find out what and how they wanted to be introduced.

The Apollo was packed. The beauty of the evening for me was, I had just learned to do an impression of Muhammad Ali and couldn't wait. The Roast started with me welcoming the people to the show and announcing who was in attendance. There was not one empty seat. Not one. Many people were standing in the back, on the sides, kneeling down. While looking out in the audience I saw many celebrities and professional ball players. One of the first players I saw was Earl the Pearl from the New York Knicks. It was so natural for me to be there, I thought. This was where I belonged.

On stage, I talked about the roast and did several of my impressions. I had the entire audience with me. They were having a good time. When it was time to bring Mr. Ali on, he stood behind the curtain next to the podium where I was standing. He was about 2-3 feet away. As I was about to introduce him I looked at him and said something to the effect of "Mr. Ali, before I bring you out, I want to share my tribute to you." He raised his eyebrows, widened his eyes and watched as I proceeded to do my impression of him. When I was done, he stepped to me, raised my hand and said he had never seen a woman do an impression of him. The audience rose to their feet.

"You doin' me? A woman doin' me? That's awesome!"

Garrett Morris, the first Black guy to appear on Saturday Night Live ("SNL") and one of the funniest people I'd seen, roasted the champ and the crowd roared. When the roast was over, he asked if he could speak with me. He was impressed because I got a standing ovation. "I want you to meet Lorne Michaels, the producer of Saturday Night Live because he is going to love what you do! You're like the 8th Wonder of the World!"

I gave him my contact number and didn't have to wait long because Garrett kept his word. Mr. Michaels was ready to meet me. He was sending a limousine to pick me up that following week.

SATURDAY NIGHT LIVE

When I got to the NBC studios I had no clue how huge this was. Garrett took me to Mr. Michaels' office. I sat down with him while Garrett listened. Mr. Michaels told me that I would start out with SNL as an associate writer, the first Black woman offered that position. They made no false promises but said I would also act as the office assistant. He must have known that I was wondering why I was the first Black woman offered that position.

"It's hard placing Black women on this show. It seems as though everything offends them. If you can come up with some things that aren't offensive, that would be good."

Eventually, I could submit some writings and move up with time and perhaps make appearances on the show. We never talked about money, time or hours. I didn't get a contract nor did I sign any papers. I didn't ask for any either. I didn't know how, I just believed them. I was right too because I got a call a few days later asking if I could come to the set of SNL and help Linda Ronstadt and Bob Hope's wife with their parts.

I didn't think I could do it. I was sick. I mean real sick, but had to make myself go. After all, I was working for Saturday Night Live. Me, Sylvia Bunny Traymore Morrison, from 16th and Corcoran Street, N.W. in Washington, DC was working at the studios of NBC's Saturday Night Live.

The limousine picked me up and took me to the station. Once there, I walked around the studio just to see what was going on. I saw a dressing room that had the name "John Belusi" on the door. Then there was "Dan Akroyd" and "Jane Curtin" on other doors. I was in the back familiarizing myself.

Before I knew it, Shebah along with Rasheeda and her boyfriend who looked like they owned NBC walked in. The two of them had on matching floor length mink coats. They were impressed but acted as if it was no big deal and appeared bored. I laughed because I knew that they were excited, otherwise they would not have come.

I met Mrs. Hope and Linda Ronstadt. I was happy to be there. Although I was sick I couldn't wait to talk to Larry to tell him my good fortune. He was going to be in Philadelphia that weekend and asked me to meet him there. I couldn't wait.

I drove and got there around 10:00 that night. I knocked on the hotel room door. No answer. I knocked again. He cracked the door but didn't let me in. "Go downstairs and wait at the bar. I'll be right down."

He closed the door. That was weird I thought. The first thing that came to my mind was he had another woman in the room. I knocked back on the door to ask him and he hurriedly said, "do like I said, I'll be right down" and shut the door.

I went downstairs and waited in the lobby. I didn't want to sit at the bar because I didn't drink. After about an hour, I went back upstairs but the same thing happened. He cracked the door and told me he was busy and would be right down. He knew I was frustrated, but wanted me to trust him. He promised he was coming down. I went back downstairs, and by the time the bar closed I had had enough. I went back upstairs and demanded that he let me in. He gave me my rules and regulations before letting me all the way in the suite.

"I'm gonna let you in, but don't repeat anything that you see. Don't say a word to anyone in this room and mind your business."

When I turned the corner I saw many guys in the room, all professional basketball players. I was the only girl, so that ruled out that he was having an orgy. They were having the biggest get high party in the world! When one of the players offered me a joint full of a little bit of everything from marijuana to cocaine to hash to whatever else, Larry got angry and told everybody to leave because he was tired and ready to go to sleep. He knew I did not get high at all. We must have stayed up the whole night talking about a little bit of everything. He left that next day.

A couple of days later, he sent for me to come back to San Antonio. We talked and laughed, went out for dinner, watched television and chilled.

He was everything I wanted in a man. I stayed for a couple of days but had to get back to work. He had games so we parted again.

This time when I got back, I was frightened because I got sick all of a sudden. I couldn't get up out of the bed. Any and everything was making me sick. The smell of foods made me almost throw up. When NBC called me in for another take, I couldn't go. I was in tears I was so sick. I had no energy and I was nauseous with headaches. I heard someone on television talking about mononucleosis.

The symptoms of mono sounded similar to mine, so I diagnosed myself with that and knew I had to get to a doctor right away. I tried to go to the hospital the next day but literally couldn't get out of bed. Larry called told me to keep him posted. He didn't like the sound of mono.

I was able to get out of the bed the next day, but had to sit down every minute or so. I took a cab to the emergency room. They took my vitals and did all kinds of tests. After a while the doctor called me in, sat me down and congratulated me. I was pregnant. Lord have mercy.

What was I going to tell Larry? I decided I wouldn't tell him. It would ruin our relationship. I broke down and cried. What was I going to do? I was sick and couldn't think right. I told Shebah who screamed with delight! Yeah right.

"Have you told Larry?"

"Of course not and I'm not going to tell him."

"You have to tell him. It is not your right to keep that information away from him."

I can't tell him. It will change the face of our relationship."

"The baby has a right to know its father. It is imperative that you tell him."

Larry called to see how I was doing but I couldn't bring myself to tell him the first time or two. He asked me what the doctors said about my condition. I broke down, in tears and told him I was pregnant. There was a long silence. He hung up the phone.

I was already sick, didn't feel good, couldn't think right and was hurt that he hung up the phone. I called him back. He told me he didn't want any babies and his religion didn't believe in abortions so I'd better do what I needed to do. What in the world did that mean? He slammed the phone down again.

I was still sick and started grieving about my parents. Maybe I should keep the baby? Maybe this baby might help my secret grieving? I started liking the little person growing in me but I was so sick I decided I would have the abortion just to get rid of the sickness. I made the appointment and worried myself the whole while I waited.

THE ABORTION

I signed in at the clinic at 3:00 pm, filled out all of the forms and met with a therapist. For about an hour, this White woman, with short light brown hair and blue eyes, asked me all kinds of questions about the baby, my future and how I felt. She spoke quietly as if she didn't want anyone to hear. She was also kind and looked at me with sad eyes.

She held the paperwork on top of her lap where her legs were crossed while she sat back in the chair. It was as if I saw here shaking her head no. The light was dim. It was like night time. The room made me sad. I think the therapist was sad too. I don't think she enjoyed her job, that's just my opinion, but I believe she wanted to help me decide what was best for me. She never smiled or frowned. She asked questions in one of the kindest voices I had ever heard. Some of the questions made me cry.

"Do you miss your parents?"

"Yes, I miss them so bad. I sometimes think that this baby is replacing some of the love I miss in them. I know it won't replace them, but some of the grief eases up when I think of it."

"Do you want to keep the baby?"

"Yes. I really do. I love it already. But, I'm so sick I can hardly breathe. Being nauseous is no joke and I have no energy whatsoever to do anything."

"How does the father feel about you and the pregnancy?"

"He's one of the reasons why I'm doing this. We initially had a really good relationship but he's a professional basketball player and thought it mighty strange I came up pregnant so early in the relationship. I got pregnant the first night. He doesn't want the baby but doesn't want me to have an abortion either. That's just crazy if you ask me. I know his religion doesn't believe in abortions but he is just as confused as me."

After the therapy session, another employee took me in a room and had me to change into what I considered "abortion" clothes. Everything I put on was white, robe and slippers included. The bed had stirrups for your feet as if you were going to be examined. It seemed like a room for surgery. It had the smell of an intensive care unit or maybe a military unit after war like the smell of blood.

It was a quiet room, an empty room. No color, no personality. There was just the bed and utensils. To me it was a death room. I could hear the silence. If you weren't already sick, you would be while lying there looking and thinking about death. In just a few moments death would take place in this room. I will have killed my baby. I shook my head side to side. This is insane, but I must summon the courage to do this. I gotta do it. Can I do it? Should I do it? I was so confused.

I was about to destroy and kill my child. I had to try to think of something else because I was getting scared, more nauseous and devastated. The young woman saw my tears. She knew I didn't like it at all. I just needed to do this and get it over with. Rest my mind and get out of sick mode. I was tired of being nauseous. Besides, I had a dynamic career ahead of me.

She left and a few minutes later a "doctor" came in the room, pulled a chair up to the bed and I got sicker. The tears started to flow because I didn't really want to do this, but I had no choice. He looked at me for a moment, said his piece and left the room. I couldn't believe what he told me.

"We are unable to perform the abortion today because we need for you to think about it. If you still want to do this after you think about it, come back."

I went into hysterics because it was imperative that they do the abortion that day.

"Come back? You're kidding right? If you don't perform the procedure today, I won't come back!"

That was the very reason they were not going to do it. They wanted me to take time to think about it and be sure. The doctor walked out of the room. I got up, put on my clothes and walked out too. I never went back.

I didn't hear back from Larry for about a month. He wanted to know the status of my pregnancy.

"They wouldn't give me the abortion."

He hung up the phone. I broke down crying. I understood his anger. I felt like I could hardly breathe. How on God's earth would I be able to tell him that I already had an abortion before this? How could I tell him that shortly after that I had a miscarriage as well? In my mind the miscarriage was a result of having the abortion in the first place. How could I have another abortion? I would never, ever be able to live with myself.

I went back to New York and tried to perform but I was too sick so I went back to DC. I didn't care about anything. I couldn't even go back to work for SNL. I needed to be near my family.

It would be 5 months or so before I would see Larry again. I learned the Spurs were playing the Bullets that coming weekend at the Capital Center. I summoned the courage to drive to the hotel. My heart sank to my stomach when I saw him and some woman come in the door. He took her to his room and came out to the lobby to see me.

"Goodness gracious. Look how big you are!" I was huge, 7 1/2 months pregnant.

"You sure you're having the baby in December because it looks like you are about to deliver the baby right now. Look, I know the baby is not mine because the timing is not right."

I knew I had not been with anyone other than him during that time and months before then. Besides, I met him in mid-March and the baby was due in December. He didn't believe me because he said that I submitted to him the first night and I had probably done that with a bunch of men. I believe he saw in my eyes that that was not true. He reached down and felt my stomach.

"Suppose it's a girl?"

He asked that because he already had a daughter and wanted a son.

"You think it's a boy?"

I started seeing hints of the old Larry I knew.

"Here's my number. Call me and let me know how things are going. I want you to keep in touch okay? I miss you."

He kissed me on my cheek and told me to take care of myself. He left me in the lobby and went to his room where the other girl was waiting. I just sat there in the quiet, me and my huge stomach. The lump left my throat and I left the hotel. There's no way I was going to call him but it didn't matter because he started calling me. He talked me into enjoying him again. We laughed and joked almost every day. I started feeling better but I was pissed off because I was absolutely crazy about him.

I easily looked as if I was carrying twins. The night of December 11, 1979, around 7:30 pm the first pain hit. I was staying with Poochie. She and the entire apartment complex were at a neighborhood meeting, leaving me home alone.

The first pain knocked me off the couch. I screamed because I had no idea what to expect. I thought when Daddy poured the alcohol in and around my eye was painful. No comparison. I thought of my friend Diane, Peter's girlfriend who had given birth to my niece Sunsearaya a month before. I went to the hospital to be with her while she was delivering so I could see what was going on. I thought death itself was in her delivery room. The pain had her screaming unmercifully. It was a really bad delivery and I was scared out of my wits.

Raymond just so happened to stop by and took me to the hospital. The doctor that examined me said I could go back home if I wanted. I was only 2 centimeters. It would be a while before I delivered. The pains were so horrible I asked what I could take to help me. They told me nothing. It was still early in the delivery process.

I couldn't go home. I had no way to get there and I had no way to get back to the hospital. I was too big in my pregnancy to drive myself.

I stayed at the hospital in labor the entire night, struggling with pain. They never gave me an epidural because I didn't have insurance. Years later I was told that Columbia Hospital, in Georgetown, Washington, DC was sued for not giving women like me extended pain medication because of the insurance issue.

Around midnight, the pains started attacking each other. The only thing I could do was reach into the air, for what, I don't know. That type of madness went on for about six hours. Sometime around 7:00 a.m. I was in a delirious state. There was no way, I believed, women endured that kind of pain and had more babies. I knew for a fact right then and there that I would never, ever have another baby.

I suffered through the night by myself. Nobody was there with me.

At 8:30 a.m. I was completely out of my mind. Each contraction delivered a deadly blow. Crying was not an option. I needed all of my strength to prepare for the next round of madness. God had to really be angry to put this kind of pain in a woman. I begged for pain medication but nobody responded to my requests. It actually felt like my back was cracking wide open.

8:45 a.m. What on God's earth is going on? I would take 10 of my mother's whippings instead of this. The pains were coming in 1-2 minute intervals. I was so delirious I didn't even realize that someone was taking me from one room to another. Everything in me was focused on dealing with the next blow of pain. I needed somebody to get that baby out.

In my delirious state, there were several people working on and around me. They tied me to the bed. HAVE THEY LOST THEIR MINDS! I can't move and oh my God! Another contraction? The doctor examined my stomach.

"I am going to check you during one of your contractions."

He had to be kidding me. I would have objected but I was too delirious. I can't tell you the level of horror I experienced as a result of that doctor examining me with no pain medication. I almost couldn't breathe, again. I couldn't say a word.

On December 12, 1979, at 9:24 am, my baby was born. The relief was unspeakable. I took a deep breath and closed my eyes to prepare for the stitch process. It didn't even matter to me that they were giving me no medication in order to proceed with the stitches. Nothing could match the level of pain I had just experienced.

The doctor asked after it was over, was it really that bad. I didn't answer. I had nothing to say to him because they could have given me something.

I was hoping it was a boy for Larry's sake but when I heard the doctors say it was a big 8 pound 11 ounce baby girl, I didn't care. They handed me my baby and the tears rolled. I was overwhelmed when I saw her. She was the most beautiful baby I had ever seen. My heart woke up that day, and through the delivery my life changed forever. The baby added a whole new dimension and I knew that we would be okay. I smiled and welcomed her in the world.

There was no one there to say hi to her with me, no one to say congratulations and no one to say how beautiful she was. No one to tell me I did a good job. No Larry to say anything, no one there, period. I cried uncontrollably not knowing if it was out of happiness or sadness. The tears would not stop. At that moment, I thought about my own mother. I would have done anything to say thank you to her. Did she have to go through something similar to what I went through all night? I wanted to thank her for everything she did for me.

I named my baby Jasmin.

I can sit here and say I didn't care, but I did care how Larry would react. They were in Los Angeles to play the Lakers. I called him. He was asleep. He heard my voice and got quiet. He knew why I was calling.

"What did you have – a boy or a girl?"

"A girl."

He hung up the phone. I was too tired and exhausted to give the emotional pain any attention.

After leaving the hospital, I went back to Poochie's apartment. Cashana, Poochie's 2 year old was one of the cutest little girls in the world. She loved Jasmin and wanted so badly to be her mother. I was never so touched in my life.

Two days after I was home, I got sick with fever. Jasmin would not drink mother's milk. I went to the hospital. The stitches I received right after delivery burst and infected my blood system. They kept me for a couple of days and told me if I had not come in when I did, I could have possibly died from the infection.

She was a big girl, 8 lbs. and 11 ozs. and needed plenty of food. By the time she was 2 weeks old she had already gained a couple of pounds. While I was in the hospital Poochie and one of her best friends, Frances Waugh, watched Jasmin and fed her baby cereal. Frances said "she's a big girl and the milk alone wasn't doing a thing for her so I gave her cereal and she is one happy baby!"

I stayed in the hospital too long and by the time I got back she still would not drink mother's milk. I gave her store bought milk and she could not digest it. She had to drink meat byproduct milk which in the 1980s cost $8.58 a can. I had to buy a can almost daily. I exhausted all of my funds. Larry disconnected himself and left us with no way to contact him. His plans were to X us out of the universe by pretending Jasmin didn't exist.

I went back to work. I talked to one of the lawyers regarding my situation. He suggested that we wait until the Spurs played the Bullets to serve Larry with papers which would probably make him take responsibility. It did. He decided he wanted to have a DNA test done. In 1980, DNA tests were not only unheard of, but expensive, somewhere in the neighborhood of $2,000-$3,000.

We took Jasmin to the University of Texas Medical Center for the test. I went back to DC and got a call a week or so later from Larry.

"She's mine. I got the results back and I'm going to take care of my responsibility."

Three months after I started working a temporary assignment as a legal secretary, I decided to move to California. I needed to get back to performing full time and what better way than to do it in big ol' sunny California. I started setting the wheels in motion for our move but luck was not on my side.

Exactly one day before our move and right after I sold my house, I got deathly ill and was admitted to Washington Hospital Center. I didn't know I had a hyper active thyroid condition that would keep me in the hospital for almost 2 weeks. When I got out, I went to Peter's house and camped there for a couple of weeks. The doctor suggested I not travel because of how sick I had been.

Peter's house was pretty cramped. Poochie was having a hard time paying the bills in her house so I decided to move with her until the doctors released me to travel. I didn't know living up town would change the face of my life forever.

THE NIGHTCLUBS

I attempted to work the open mike nightclubs on the weekdays in DC when I was allowed to. It was hard getting time in the mainstream clubs considering there was basically only Garvin's and the Comedy Café. Me being the only single Black Female in the area, I rarely got a chance to get on stage. Fortunately, a couple of comics liked me and started inviting me to do shows with them. Before I knew it, I was invited to the IBEX, a local club on Georgia Avenue in DC.

I wasn't sure how I would do in the Marvin Gaye Room. I had a 30 minute routine down pat with the exception of 2 newly created characters, Pink Lady and Michael Jackson at 75 years old. There may have been about 12 people in the room when I started because most people bypassed the Marvin Gaye Room and proceeded upstairs to the dance part of the club.

At the end of the set, it was packed. Ron Green, the manager, was pleased and said I was welcome anytime I wanted to come back. I got to work a lot with many DC favorites. I befriended the Hopkins Family, Catfish, several bands and various comics. Buddy, the brother in the Hopkins Family and I became good friends. Today, he is singing with the Platters.

Working the Ibex allowed me the opportunity to really pull it together. It's a good thing I tightened my act too. I was headed to the Carter Baron Amphitheatre. The way that happened was, one of DC's band leaders, Tommy Bryant, called me to do a set. Most of the time, they were doing the set for free and exposure. We were scheduled to work at the Sheraton Hotel on Connecticut Avenue.

After the set, this guy walked up to me and introduced himself as the Director for the National Park Service. He was the person responsible for bringing shows to all of the parks in the area including the Carter Baron. Every comic in DC wanted to work the Carter Baron. That is where the action was in the summer months. Anybody from Richard Pryor to the Ojays to Melba Moore would headline. He invited me to stop by the Carter Baron that coming weekend so that he could try and squeeze me in. Rarely did local comics get that opportunity. There was only one Black

Female Impressionist in the country at that time, and I was it. Al Dale thought I would be perfect for that venue.

In the meantime, I worked during the day for the Federal Government where I met Priscilla Jamison. Her family became like my second family. I left the government and moved into private industry working for a law firm as a legal secretary. Priscilla came to work with me at the law firm and so did Rona. We ended up carpooling. Another woman carpooled with us. She was a lawyer in the law firm and a good one at that. She was one of the finest people I ever met in my life. We found it shocking that a Yale law school graduate, didn't mind riding with a bunch of secretaries. She was cool.

I was the driver. Priscilla, Rona and I often speak of the "roommate" of the lawyer. Often times the lawyer would ask if I could drop her roommate at her office. She worked on Capitol Hill. This happened on a few occasions.

One day, Rona, Priscilla, the lawyer and I were laughing and talking before we dropped the roommate off. The roommate was not that friendly but we didn't know why and didn't care. She was a friend of the lawyer and any friend of hers was a friend of ours. During this time, being gay was not as popular as it is today so sadly, lots of gay people remained in the closet. When the roommate got out of the car, the lawyer got out too. Priscilla, Rona and I happened to see them kiss. The 3 of us, wide eyed and shocked, giggled because we were not accustomed to seeing 2 women kiss! I never dreamed that the roommate would end up appearing in congressional hearings regarding Judge Clarence Thomas. The lawyer was Sonia Jarvis and the roommate was Anita Hill.

THE CARTER BARON – MELBA MOORE

On August 20, 1984, at Al Dale's request, I opened for Melba Moore at the Carter Baron. DC was in love with her. Melvin Lindsey, from WHUR, the originator of the Quiet Storm, was the master of ceremonies that night. I was not on the bill and the audience didn't know who I was or what to expect. Neither did Melvin.

He introduced me and stood on the side of the stage to watch. I saw Al on the other side of the stage watching as well, hoping he made a good choice. By the end of the set, the audience was on their feet and so were the writers from the Washington Post. Congratulations were coming from everywhere and people were telling me what a great job I did. I am going to move a little ahead of myself for a minute because I have to tell you what happened the next year.

That following summer I was booked to open for Melba again since our show did well the first time. I was hoping that I would at least get a chance to meet her this time and thank her for making room for me as her opening act. I invited many family members and friends to the show that night because I was banking on that same magic to take place. To my surprise, Melvin Lindsey, the same master of ceremonies from the year before, pulled me to the side and told me that they just cancelled me off the show. Melba Moore didn't want me on the bill. She would not perform if they allowed me to go on stage in front of her. She insisted that I be taken off.

What? What did he mean? Melba Moore? Why did she not want me on the bill? I was just a little peon representing my hometown. She on the other hand, was Melba Moore, a super star. She was who everybody was there to see. It didn't matter who opened for her. She was Melba Moore. THE Melba Moore. She flat out refused to perform if they allowed me on that stage. What did I do to her? I was a respectful act and warmed the audience for the big act. Had I said something wrong, did I disrespect her in some way? What happened?

Melvin saw the tears swelling in my eyes.

"Cheer up Sylvia. It's okay. Look at it as a compliment to your talent. You're so awesome you're giving the big boys and girls a run for their money."

I tried not to be upset but I was. I don't know the truth about why she didn't want me performing that night. I didn't work with Ms. Moore and to this day I don't know the reason, but shortly after that, I was back at the Carter Baron performing with Jennifer Holiday. I remember a little guy following me all over the place backstage. Where ever I went he was right there. He was the cutest little thing and I couldn't figure out who he was there with or why he was there. After he told me that he would like for me to be his girlfriend, I couldn't help but smile. Cute little kid I thought to myself. I asked him his name and he told me, with the biggest smile he could muster. "My name is Johnny Gill."

Things were starting to happen. Next thing I knew, Dimensions Unlimited called for me to open for Chaka Kahn.

CHAKA KAHN

Chaka Kahn was headlining at the Warner Theatre in DC. That was a huge break for my career. The show was sold out and the theatre was packed and if you think Washington loves Melba Moore, you should see how they react to Chaka Kahn.

I was informed of the Chaka rules and regulations. I couldn't mention her name on stage and I couldn't be vulgar. No problem.

Chaka and another woman entered the backstage area looking a hot mess. I couldn't believe it. It's a shame we sometimes judge quickly. Now that I am older, I believe she may have looked like that as a result of being tired and exhausted from the road tour. Whatever she looked like when she came in, it all changed once the show started. I went on first and I have to admit, I love the DC audience. They do not play with you. If you are good they will acknowledge it. If not, you may want to seriously change things around. Thank goodness they liked me. I had to pause many times to let them applaud and I was humbled by their reaction. It was a real blessing to be on that show.

Chaka came out strong and there was no doubt that her voice was in full swing. There is no leopard, tiger or lion that could have walked with her on that stage. Her sexy black outfit showed shadows of her curves, and the breasts were sitting up there like two little twin cantaloupes rolling around in water waiting to jump out! Her lips were painted bright red and her make up was dark and seductive. She knew how to squint her eyes to make it seem as though she was focusing on you and you alone. Her hands were moving with the beats and her feet moved her around the stage seeming to spell "SEX!" Yes, she looked fabulous and oh my goodness, the voice. She tore that house down!

Chaka must have sung every popular song she ever made and every song in her repertoire was sung with everything she had. I'm sure she bought back a lot of memories for the audience because she sure bought back many for me. I haven't seen a performance like that in a long time and I was proud to have shared the bill with her. I met her afterward and thought she was truly regal. She was polite to each and every person who was there to meet her. That woman left a lasting impression on me and showed me what confidence was all about. I was happy the next day after reading the reviews in the Washington Post. From that day forward, I learned how not to judge entertainers no matter how worn they look. Chaka proved to me that how you looked didn't necessarily have any bearing on what you could do to an audience.

Between working the IBEX, the Carter Baron and doing a lot of one nighters, I had developed a name for myself in the DC area where people started recognizing me on the street telling me where they last saw me and how much they enjoyed the show.

Gramercy Productions, a spin off from Dimensions Unlimited called me shortly thereafter and gave me a gig that involved a short tour with Jeffrey Osborne. I had never been on a tour in the states and the salary they gave me was just enough to pay my fare to get to the venue and pay for the hotels and food. I didn't care. I was out there with one of the big boys and loved every minute of it. I chalked it up as part of the business - paying my dues.

Jeffrey Osborne was a complete gentleman. He made himself available to everyone touring with him. I think that since his songs were so heartwarming, you almost couldn't tell if he was the bomb on stage or not. While watching him perform, his likeable quality jumped out at you and you fell in love. His voice was magic and his attitude was wonderful. It was a good tour and a wonderful experience. After the tour I headed back to DC.

No sooner than I got there, Dimensions Unlimited called again. Gladys Knight and the Pips were performing in DC and needed an opening act because their regular opener couldn't be there. I got the job. I was asked to go with them to Richmond. Both shows were sold out and went extremely well. The question was posed as to whether or not they should keep me or go with their regular opening act. Because Gladys and my sister are friends, Gladys asked her what she thought. My sister, who likes to "speak her mind" and "keep it real" told Gladys "I think my sister is good, but, you should go with who you already have." I don't believe she meant any harm. Chubby was very honest about these kind of questions.

In her heart, she believed the other act was more worthy. I couldn't challenge that because that it what she believed. It just wasn't my journey. Oh, and I think the opening act at the time was Byron Allen.

PARKWOOD

Poochie's house was a complete mess. The walls needed painting, the kitchen and dining room needed a makeover and all 3 bedrooms needed work. I went straight to the furniture store, bought a bed and got some paint and anything else I could use to wake up the bedroom. When finished, no one could believe that room belonged in that house. Wicker baskets were placed on tables and the floor. I added a nice floor rug that matched the bed linen. I hung pictures and put up curtains to match, so I thought. It was pretty nice if I might say so myself.

I got sick again and was admitted to the hospital for my thyroid. I stayed a week. They wanted to surgically remove the gorge from my throat but I was too afraid to take a chance on having my vocal chords cut. The doctor said if I didn't have the surgery, I should take a once in a life time dosage of radioactive iodine. It would reduce the knot in my throat but would not allow me to have any more children. No big deal, considering what I had been through with having Jasmin. I didn't want any more kids any way so that was the perfect solution for me. I went through with the radioactive iodine treatment. In the back of my mind, I was a little uncomfortable with the idea of never, ever being able to have children.

After that hospital stay, I went back uptown. I met a lot of hustlers and drug dealers. Hustlers were nothing new to me because I grew up in the hood with many hustlers. Drug dealers and people who used drugs were fascinating. They were impressed with me because I talked different, never cursed, wore what they considered expensive clothes, drove a nice car and helped my sister get on her feet. A lot of times, they wanted to sit and talk with me in the evenings when it was too hot to be in the house. Uptown, in the ghetto, most people sat outside on their porches and watched the activity. They watched the drug dealers deal, watched the police chase the drug dealers and the people who bought the drugs, watched girls fight over guys, and watched guys fight just to prove who had authority. There were thieves, weed smokers and people who loved smoking what they called at the time, Love Boat also identified as PCP or what I understood to be embalming fluid. People were making mega money selling drugs and everybody wanted to get in. I was sort of the therapist in that area. I talked about getting jobs and trying to make a life and moving out of the hell hole they were in. None of them wanted to hear what I was saying but since it sort of made sense they listened. What everyone wanted to do was get high and make the fast street money. Unfortunately, everybody that got high couldn't stop getting high and I couldn't understand it.

Every time this one guy came around folks wanted to be around him because he knew how to freebase cocaine, similar to what Richard Pryor was allegedly doing. They were addicted to freebasing and couldn't get away from it. When they told me they couldn't help themselves, I told them if they started it, they could stop it. Quitting should be no problem.

I look back on those days realizing I had a lot of nerve talking about habits with no knowledge or experience whatsoever. I had never even smoked a cigarette (except when I was a kid and Ma made me eat them) much less smoked drugs. I didn't even drink - not even a beer let alone try to convince someone that they didn't have to do drugs.

What I'm about to tell you is something that I'm sure will raise questions because nobody does this. No one "turned me out" in the drug world. I turned myself out because I decided I would show them how to start doing drugs and then just stop, simple as that. Start. Stop. I didn't know what I was getting myself into but I was about to meet the devil himself.

THAT DEVIL AIN'T NO JOKE

The same guy, who knew how to freebase and cook cocaine stopped to talk one day. I told him I wanted to buy some cocaine.

"$50 will buy you a big ol' $50 bag."

I gave him the money. He came back about a half hour later with the coke and suggested we go to his house. He took out a little bottle with a black top, put some water and baking soda in it along with the coke and put fire to the bottom of the bottle, all the while talking too fast for me to understand what it was he was talking about. When he was through heating the bottle and bringing the ingredients to a boil, he added a little cold water and a big hard rock appeared at the bottom of the little glass bottle. He told me it was cooked. He then placed the rock on a mirror and cut it into several pieces. I knew nothing of what he was doing and had to go by what he told me.

He put a piece of the white rock in one of two of what is called a stem, which is attached to a round glass jar known as the pipe. Inside the one stem, which is glass also, were tiny pieces of "screen." Some people used the screen from out of their window to put in the stem part of the pipe. Although tiny, these little screens played an important role in accessing the heat for the melting of the cocaine. The stem contained the screen. The other stem was used to suck the smoke from out of the bowl. He took a torch, lit the stem area that housed the white piece of coke that laid on the top of the screens, put the other stem to my mouth and told me to pull. The whole round part of the jar filled with white smoke. Before I could pull it good enough for the smoke to come through the screens to me, he snatched the pipe, turned the mouth piece part to his mouth and proceeded to pull the smoke all the way through.

He pulled forever - much longer than what I had pulled. Totally different from mine, he got the best of the smoke.

After blowing the smoke out, he talked for about 5 minutes nonstop saying that the coke was good, some of the best he had. He talked a lot of gibberish. I couldn't understand a word he said. He got up, peeped out the window, went to the door to make sure it was locked, peeped through the peephole a couple of times and started feeling in his pockets. He also started looking all around the floor, for what, I don't know. After the pipe cooled down, he announced it was his turn to take his hit. His hit? He just hit the one piece he put in the pipe for me.

He put another piece of the rock in the stem, lit it and pulled until the bowl filled with white smoke. He pulled until it was almost empty. He then turned the mouthpiece to me and motioned for me to pull but by the time he finished pulling there was nothing.

"See baby girl, you don't know how to make the smoke come back. I'ma show you. You gotta know what you doin."

He cooled the stem off with an old washcloth wiping the stem until it cooled down, all the while blowing at the stem, talking more gibberish. He was looking around with eyes so big you would have thought he saw a ghost. He took a clothes hanger, bent it until it was straight, wrung it around and around until it broke, and pushed the little screens down to the other end of the stem and inserted the detachable stem back in the bowl. He relit the torch, placed the heat to the stem and sure enough made the smoke come back.

After the bowl cleared, he blew the smoke out, turned the mouthpiece to me and again motioned for me to pull. Of course nothing came through the bowl because he had pulled it all. He just shook his head. "See, you don't know what you doing." He started talking more gibberish, looking out the peephole, and hiding behind one of the windows constantly peeking out to see if anybody was there. He kept saying he had to watch out for the police. He packed up his equipment and said he had to go.

"What about the rest of the coke?"

"Rest of what coke? We smoked it all!"

I couldn't argue with him at the time because I didn't know any better. He took advantage of me not knowing and if I did know, I couldn't prove it. I went home trying to figure out what happened to my $50, but it was important to me to get this habit so that I could show these folks. He came back later, saying he had more coke and took me to a friend of his.

We went to a house not too far from where he and I lived and the guy who lived there asked was I a policeman because I was too clean to be "one of them." My friend told them, no, I was almost a star. He told him that I worked the club circuit and appeared all over the city. He also told the guy that I had money which instantly let the guy know to treat me good. He assumed that eventually, I would be back. There happened to be several people in that house that evening, all of whom had a package of coke. A few people gave me a piece and I finally got a chance to get all of the white smoke in the bowl. I cannot describe for you what I personally felt, but it was different, good. I didn't get high like I did the first time I tried marijuana. The marijuana made me hungry and sleepy. I liked the cocaine and eventually forgot the reason why I was doing it.

The next couple of days, I bought my own $50 packages and invited all kinds of people to get high with me. I didn't know that coke was not a social drug. People will hurt or kill you for it, depending on the situation. I didn't know any of this. It got to be expensive so I had to let that whole social scene go. I found myself buying a bag almost daily, sometimes 2 or 3 bags a day. I had a habit. Lucky me.

BACK TO SAN ANTONIO

I was glad Larry and I had a decent relationship. Although he only visited DC maybe 2 or 3 times a year, he kept in touch, sent Jasmin boxes and was doing the best he could long distance.

I was spiraling out of control on the drugs. It had come to a point where I didn't care how I looked, dressed or the fact that I was weighing around 99 pounds. The only time I half way cared is when I had a gig that forbid me to look any old kind of way. People started talking about how I was letting myself go.

One night I spent every dime I had, every dime. I believe it was the most impacting night I had in that demonic world. I cried for hours and picked up the phone and called Larry in San Antonio. I revealed to him that I had a drug habit. He sympathized and sent me a ticket to come to San Antonio with him. He picked me up at the airport and wanted to know how this happened? I was one of the only women he knew that didn't even drink wine. He suggested I get some rest and not to worry. He left out. I slept upstairs alone. He didn't tell me that he was getting married. On a phone conversation during that time, his wife to be told me that after having 2 children, they felt the right thing to do would be for him to marry her.

When Larry returned around 6:00 am the next morning he was a monster, totally different from the night before. "Get yo behind up out of that bed – you are not at a resort. I can't believe you talked me into spending money to fly you down here. You better find a way to pay me back and figure out a way to get back home." I couldn't believe how he changed overnight. He looked different too. He laid down for a few hours and woke up totally different again, nice this time. I knew something was wrong.

After making sure I ate, he told me he would be back. When he returned the old monster was back. He started yelling about how I was there and I should not be there and he didn't want me there.

"You need to leave now!"

He left out and didn't come back until the next day raging.

"Larry, are you getting high?"

"Mind yo' business." He was quite touchy.

I couldn't take the ups and downs of Larry the monster so I asked if he could send me home. He must have felt bad because he started trying to console me, but I had to get back home to get Jasmin and didn't want to continue on the roller coaster.

I was hanging out at Tracey's. A tall attractive woman she dated a guy who could get drugs whenever he wanted. Her place was where I could go and be assured to get high. No matter what time of day I knocked on her door, she opened it. I often went to 14th and Spring Place in Northwest Washington to get high but if you didn't have anything to share with the keeper of the house, you had to go.

I was back on the coke scene and on it hard, until I got a call from a woman named Gwen at Gramercy Productions.

WHITNEY INTRO

June 2, 1985. I was home playing a game of spades (a card game) with several friends when the phone rang. One of my neighbors, Jo Jo Waller, answered the phone. I quickly motioned him that I was unavailable to take the call. The card game was intense and I was just getting over one of my 3 day binges on coke. He was listening to the voice on the other end and put his hand over the mouthpiece and said it was Gramercy Productions wanting to know if I could get to the Warner Theater to open for Whitney Houston. Whitney was one of the biggest acts in the country and was working off a platinum album. Everybody loved this woman and it was clearly an opportunity I should not miss. I grabbed the phone and was told the original comic, Andy Evans, who was scheduled to open the show, may have thought the engagement was Saturday night. The show was starting at 8:00 and it was already 7:30. If I could get there on stage around 8:00 they would throw in an extra bonus. I told them I could do it.

I changed into a pair of size 4 tight black leggings with a sparkling long gold tank top and gold 3 inch high heels. I hopped in a cab, took the rollers out of my hair, put on my make-up, all while riding in the cab. I was able to walk on stage at 8:05 pm. Gramercy Productions loved it.

The Warner Theatre was packed, standing room only. This was Whitney's preparation engagement for an upcoming tour as a result of her first big album which included "You Give Good Love" and "I'm Saving All My Love For You."

The announcer simply introduced the opening act by saying "please welcome to the stage, from Washington, DC, Comedienne Sylvia Traymore." The audience could have cared less. I recognized that and knew that I would have to make the next half hour mean something. I walked out on the stage hoping I would do well because I had to. The audience, most of whom didn't know who I was, sat there quietly waiting to see who I was. One thing about most DC audiences, they give you approximately 1 minute to determine whether or not they like you. If you come off not so well, you will know it. After 30 seconds, I could hear laughter and saw people paying attention. It was like a wave of loud talking converting to a wave of silence so that everyone could hear. It startled me at first. After about 5 minutes all eyes were directly on the performance. I was, in my mind, thanking God the whole while, happy that the audience responded by giving me 3 standing ovations. "Bless them" I thought quietly. I wished I could take each and every one of them and hide them in my pocket for my next engagement!

After a short intermission it was time for Whitney. You could feel the energy of excitement in the air. People were arranging themselves in their seats because they knew they were in for a treat.

The minute she walked on the stage people were on their feet. They clapped, screamed, jumped up and down, hollered Whitney's name, cried, shouted, waved and whatever else they could think of. Some people simply stood there with their hands clasped under their chins. She delivered a stellar performance. Washington loved her. So did I.

After the show, I went to meet Whitney, a little something I do when I open for someone. She was sweating profusely, but in all of that she was polite but very tired. I understood. She met and greeted everyone who came to see her and then made a mad getaway.

The Washington Post article on June 3, 1985 was awesome. It expressed how the hometown crowd was devastated by "Sylvia" with brash impressions of Diana Ross and Dionne Warwick and ended it suggesting that a shot at Star Search and an upcoming tour with Irene Cara would finally bring the type of national exposure that Sylvia deserved. Deserved? They thought that? I was ecstatic.

Mr. Houston, Whitney's father, thought I was an excellent opening and suggested they use me for future performances. He got my phone number and said that they would call. In this business, people usually give you their number to call them. I didn't expect to hear from him. I was wrong.

I got a call to see if I could come to Newark to perform at a fundraiser for the mayoral candidate Mr. Houston was working for. Whitney was headlining and I would serve as her opening act.

The Houston organization (which is what I called Whitney and her Dad sometimes) made all of my flight and hotel arrangements. They also sent a limo to the airport to pick me up when I arrived and took me to the theatre. Inside the theatre, many people were in the wings watching me because I got out of a limousine and they figured I had to be somebody.

I didn't know anyone there. There was no one with me either. Alone, I didn't have an assistant to help me get dressed or carry my bags. I had no one to give instructions on how to set up my stage or play music. No one to talk to about how excited I was or to calm me down. I was one little tiny entity. A nobody with an opportunity. A super opportunity and to be honest, I could have cared less that I was alone and by myself. Shucks, I was getting ready to open for Whitney Houston again!

The mc asked if I was ready. He saw my excitement. The Newark audience was quiet. I believe they were respectful because it was a fundraiser. I explained to them how delighted I was to be there and hoped they enjoyed the show. I love Newark. They gave up 3 standing ovations. You could still hear the audience loudly stirring once I left the stage which was a good indication that they thoroughly enjoyed it.

I couldn't wait to get a good standup spot backstage to watch Whitney. I didn't care where I was as long as I could see the show.

She came out on the stage like a princess! Stunning, mesmerizing, over the top, beautiful and sung like she just left Heaven. She was sparkling all over the place and held a small handkerchief to wipe her forehead whenever she sweated. The concert was not only sold out it was a huge success. They told me they were pleased at my performance and convinced I should go on the first tour.

The tour was all I thought about. Several months later, I learned the tour was already in place. They were using an act from Star Search. I was devastated but after I thought about it, who was I? I didn't have any hit records, albums or concerts that put me over the top. No extraordinary empires connected with my name. Nobody knew me and nobody outside of Washington, DC cared. Shucks, I was probably lucky to get what I did when I got it. Who the heck was Sylva Traymore Morrison?

STAR SEARCH

Garvin's in Washington, DC was sponsoring the Star Search auditions and chose approximately 19 acts to be seen.

It was a fun time and an opportunity that all 19 of us were excited about. Many of the 19 went on to have lucrative careers. Tony Perkins became the weather man for Good Morning America and is now on Foxx News in the morning, Tommy Davidson, (most of you know him from his In Living Color fame), Chris Thomas who became BET's Mayor of Rap City, Jeff Penn hires and fires a lot of entertainment names, Bill King, Bob Somersby, who that night had a couple of his college roommates in the audience – Vice President Al Gore and actor Tommy Lee Jones, Andy Evans, the Comedy Counselor, helped write an HBO special for Wanda Sykes and worked with Martin Lawrence and Dave Chappelle, Vincent Cook, who now does movies with Will Smith and is most known for his role as Muhammad Ali, the hit play that is touring the country, Ed Wilsinski, Ron Moranian, Daniel Russ, Bill McCuddy, Greg Poole and Brett Leake. There was also Marla Aaron, the only White Female Comic in the competition. And then there was me. I was number 3 in the lineup for the tryouts.

Sinbad was there and told me he was sure I secured a spot. I didn't stay around for the rest of the auditions. I went home to wait on my call.

I didn't have any night club work so I took on a temporary legal secretarial assignment to help defray some of the costs associated with performing and also to help pay some of my bills.

I decided to take an early lunch one day at work. I use to kid around with the secretaries telling them if Bill Cosby or Muhammad Ali called, tell them not to call me anymore, just joking of course.

When I returned from lunch, one of the girls laughed at me saying,

"Oh Sylvia, John Houston who said he's Whitney Houston's father called. He left a number and said for you to call him."

She walked on as if it was a big joke. I knew it was not a joke because of the area code associated with the number. My heart started pounding because I knew he was not just calling to say hello.

This was a business call.

WHITNEY 2

I called. Mr. Houston asked if I could be in New York that evening in time for a 7:30 performance to open for Whitney. I quickly calculated that if I left right then and there at 2:15, made it to the airport to catch the 4:00 shuttle, I could be in NY at 5:00, hop in a cab and be at the venue in good time.

I called the temporary agency and told them I was leaving the assignment and to cancel all future assignments. I wondered where my air and cab fare and spending money was coming from. Thank God for Poochie. She gave me all of the money she had and I made a mental note not to forget. It was enough to get to the New York venue. They would reimburse me for my expenses allowing for spending money.

Between the traffic and my excitement, I didn't know what to do with myself. Suppose I was no good? Suppose the audience didn't like me? What if this was one of those nights I didn't perform well? All kinds of thoughts were going through my head. I didn't know what to expect. How big of an audience would it be? Who else was on the show? Would there be someone there to play my music?

The cab dropped me off at the most beautiful amphitheater. It was sitting outside on water. I thought to myself with a smile. Thank you God, this is the BIG TIME.

Whitney's "people" greeted and welcomed me and took me to my dressing room which was awesome. I thought about the little hallway dressing rooms I had been in back at the IBEX in DC and some of the other places I performed in at home and it was nothing like this. I had fruit, chips, mini snacks, a whole barrel of drinks which consisted of beer, sodas, alcohol, juice, you name it. There were mirrors and lights everywhere just like a big star's dressing room.

Prior to the actual show, they told me my dos and don'ts. I had 30 minutes on stage and depending on how my set turned out would determine if I would continue with the tour. They said to me that Whitney was America's sweetheart and she marketed mainly to young White females. They made it clear that I should not in any way form or fashion insult that group. They must have forgotten that I had the cleanest, funniest, entertaining act in the business. I was like a combination of Bill Cosby and Sammy Davis, Jr. – female version. People could bring their kids to see me and everyone would be entertained. Their requirements were not a problem.

At 7:30 pm sharp, the MC started the show from backstage introducing me. I aggressively walked on stage determined to win the audience and prove to all of management that I was their girl.

The sound from the microphone was magnificent. You could hear an ant walking. I started my act explaining that I use to be an airline stewardess and what your flight would be like if all of your flight attendants were stars. I asked them if they could imagine taxiing down the runway listening to somebody like Lily Tomlin making the announcements. Back in the day, and still today, Lily Tomlin was one of the finest comics/entertainers in the business and most White people knew who she was. In my set, Ernestine, one of Tomlin's characters, would introduce other stars on the flight which included Dionne Warwick, who introduced Diana Ross and I'd take it from there. Cher was on the show as one of my impressions and so were Nancy Wilson and Patti LaBelle. I closed the set with a power rendition of Tina Turner singing Proud Mary. In the Tina Turner routine, I usually went into the audience and randomly selected a guy to play the part of Ike and most times got a standing ovation for my impression of Tina Turner. This time, although the audience loved it, I didn't get a standing ovation.

When I left that stage fully out of breath from working so hard to please them, I got nervous. Did they roar and scream that hard because they were really entertained or were they glad to get me off stage so that Whitney could come on? But what if management didn't like me? Suppose they sent me home? This was terrible. I wish someone would say something.

It didn't matter at that moment because the lights dimmed, the breeze subsided and the thousands of people went crazy. Whitney Houston was about to take the stage. I was backstage when she walked past me and she was absolutely beautiful.

Up close she was more beautiful in person than any camera could ever project. Tall, elegant, a body to die for, every hair on her head in place, flawless skin, piercing eyes and a smile to warm your heart, she had it all. Before she walked out on the stage, she gathered folks around her and prayed - giving all of the praise to God. I cried. She was absolutely beautiful, humble and magical - and I was standing right there watching.

You could hardly hear her first song because of the crowd. She created an atmosphere where she owned each and every person there. Her mere presence was spellbinding and she was the most humble person I had ever seen on stage. The audience quieted down after her first song and let her talk. The rest of the show was unbelievable. All Whitney had to do was stand there and sing and that's exactly what she did. I was still standing there in awe when she left the stage and couldn't believe how much power this woman had on stage, but now it was time for business. My fate was at stake. Plus it was time to get paid.

Whitney walked by and said "Great show." Did she see my show? She must have because she said great show. For real? Great show? Those words kept repeating themselves in my head until I couldn't remember exactly how she said them. Was it GREAT SHOW with emphasis on the word great or GREAT SHOW with emphasis on the word SHOW? Did she mean that she was about to have a great show or did she mean I had a great show? I got way too excited because Whitney said great show! She must have seen me. Must have! Oh my God she said great show! She liked me! Would Whitney have the last word on whether or not I stayed? Did she like me? Was I good enough? I kept thinking "Please God, let her like me, please."

When all was done at the show that night the limos took us back to the hotel and I signed for my room. When I got settled I heard a lot of noise in the hallway. There was a woman out there screaming to the top of her lungs. I looked through the peep hole and it looked like Whitney. Like any sensible nosey person I grabbed the ice bucket and headed for the vending area because I wanted to see what was going on. When I opened the door, there was Whitney literally dragging a woman out of the room across from mine. She was telling her that nobody was going to ruin her tour with drugs. I couldn't believe that was Whitney Houston in a home girl hoochie/ghetto mode. She had my respect right then and there. I laughed to myself because I thought what would I have done? I had never been in a fight in my life and here this woman was handling her business. She had a keen eye of what most people were doing and she was not going for any foolishness. She put the woman out and apologized to me for her behavior and walked away. I was thinking "Whitney don't play!"

I was given my own limousine and driver, so to speak and all expenses were taken care of. In return I was on time for every performance and did everything I could to be the perfect opening act. Everyone seemed pleased with my personal and professional attitude and performance. I was accustomed to standing ovations and since I was not getting them on the tour, I knew something was wrong. They liked my performance but not enough to stand up. There had to be something I could do to get a standing ovation from these audiences. We had a few days off from the tour which allowed me the opportunity to go home and work on changing my set. I took the closing part of my act, which was the strongest and used it as the opening. It was the best move I could have made. The first night back out on the tour, I opened the set with my impression of Tina Turner and the audience went bananas. They were on their feet. Raves from Whitney's management and the press kind of let me know I was in. I was glad I changed my set around.

One night in Canada, after a spectacular performance, I got a standing ovation. Near the end of Whitney's set, she sent security to look for me and motioned me to come on stage with her. At first I didn't want to go because I didn't know what to expect. Had I done something wrong? Did she want me to see something? Was I in trouble? Did she want to make a special announcement? None of the above.

What she did was, grabbed my hand, held it high in the air with hers, and I believe you could hear the roar of the audience for miles. While they were going nuts, Whitney looked at me, winked her eye and smiled. I knew she was pleased. We left the stage and before security could take either of us away from the stage, we gave each other a big hug. Whitney was the absolute biggest thing in the industry at that time, and she was delighted with having me on her tour. I went back to my dressing room, broke down and cried. Whitney Houston selflessly shared her stage with me. No one told her to do that. I often think of that noble moment and thank her for that to this day.

The final leg of the tour was in Los Angeles, California for 4 nights where any and everybody were in the audience. I was told Berry Gordy, Dionne Warwick, Diana Ross and many others including Michael Jackson, were there. The nights were all about the hottest female act in the country - Whitney Houston. Many of the big names didn't necessarily care to see the opening act, but once they heard the commotion, most of them came in the venue to see what was going on. Some people wanted to know who I was and where I came from.

After one of the performances in Los Angeles, this really gorgeous woman came to my dressing room to tell me how much she enjoyed my show. She looked awfully familiar but I couldn't place her face. She had a calm fun spirit and laughed about the show and how awesome she thought I was. The more we talked the more familiar she became. As I was about to ask her where I knew her from, she introduced herself. It was Natalie Cole. Natalie asked why I was not doing an impression of her, all the while smiling. I told her I was working on it. I love Natalie and was honored she stopped to say hello to me.

One night on a leg of the tour Whitney invited me and all the ladies associated with the tour to ride on her bus with her. She and I must have talked the whole bus ride. She told me about her housekeeper, whose name was Sylvia (my eyes kind of squinted when she said that and we both laughed.) We talked about concepts and what it was like getting started in the business. With over 75 people connected with the tour, there were approximately 8 women all together. I was the one lone act and you couldn't tell me anything. I was sitting there becoming good friends with Whitney Houston.

The next day, she and I went shopping. I went to buy some stage clothes and shoes, satisfied that there would be no problem paying for it. I was making good money. Whitney went shopping just because. She had me buying all kinds of designer sunshades and outfits that I would have never purchased if I was alone. After all, I couldn't imagine how much money she was making. There were ticket sales, pictures, paraphernalia, tee shirts and anything and everything Whitney. It was madness.

Another night while in Los Angeles, I was pleasantly surprised to see my good friend Dewey Hughes. After the show, he told me how proud he was of me.

"While you were performing I couldn't get over the fact that in just a short while, the fabulous Whitney Houston, herself, would be gracing that stage." He was even more surprised and shocked that I was there under no management or contract. How could that be? He was impressed that I was on that tour but not happy about the fact that I had no contract. He was happy that I got in.

While in Los Angeles, I also ran into Tommy Davidson. Tommy was auditioning for the hit sitcom "In Living Color" and based on his performances in the Washington DC area there was no question in my mind that he would do well in the industry.

Whitney performed under some harsh conditions in Los Angeles. It was so cold her first night she had to sing in a suede coat. Although her throat was getting hoarse, she was determined to give the people everything she had. I wish people really knew the Whitney I know. She is funny, friendly and caring. More importantly, she loves God. She prayed before every performance. If the tour broke for a week or two and her entire crew went home, she still paid their salary. She would give you the shirt off her back. Just don't get her wrong.

There was a little girl backstage with a group of people waiting to meet Whitney. This little girl was a part of the "Make A Wish Foundation" which involves terminally ill patients hoping to meet their favorite artist while they are still living. The only thing this particular little girl wanted to do before she died was meet Whitney.

When they presented the little girl to Whitney, she did everything she could to not cry. She cried in her dad's arms, just saying over and over "why Daddy, why?" It was so moving I think all of us cried.

The tour proved to be so successful that Billboard listed the tour, with just Whitney and I, in the no.1 or no. 2 spot almost the entire summer.

In late August, 1986, the U.S. tour came to an end. When I thought about it, I met a lot of cool people, one of which was Ricky Minor, who was Whitney's bass player at the time, but is now one of the biggest names in the music industry catering to such shows as the music director for American Idol, many BET specials and almost every major awards show that graces television. Later in the years, Ricky was always available whenever I needed to get backstage for a performance he was involved in. What a super guy.

After the tour, I went back home and stayed with Poochie who by that time moved to Maryland away from all of the uptown drama. I got a call from Larry who told me that he had been thinking about me and Jasmin and the future and decided that he would not be coming to see Jasmin anymore. He didn't want me calling for anything and wanted me to pretend that I never knew him.

"Find Jasmin another father and forget that I exist." He hung up the phone. I had no opportunity to ask why or anything.

What was this all about? What was wrong? What happened? What was he talking about? What had I done? Why would he, after 6 years, decide that he didn't want to have anything else to do with her? What had she done? I just couldn't get that out of my mind. He changed his numbers, didn't call and kept his word. He never came back to see Jasmin. Never called or nothing. Never.

I couldn't worry about him at that moment. I had to keep my focus on my career and hope that whatever changes he was going through at the time would end soon. I had just finished a major tour and had to keep it moving. I was almost there, almost.

I started calling people that showed interest. A company that represents key entertainers like Bill Cosby expressed interest. The word on the street was that I was the next big thing in the business. They would get back with me with more information.

A couple of weeks went by and I became concerned that I hadn't heard from them. I decided to call and was shocked when they told me they were no longer interested. All of a sudden you have no interest whatsoever? They almost signed me over the telephone when we first talked. What happened? I tried a couple of other companies to get some work and they almost hung up in my face. What in the world was going on?

Did this have something to do with me exposing some illegal money trading that took place while I was on the road that I don't care to discuss now for fear of my life? I'm still afraid of that incident, even to this day. There was no way I could come off a tour like that, with all of the write ups, interviews and performances I did and not be in position to continue with a fabulous career. I knew something was wrong but dared not try to do anything about it, for fear of being murdered for exposing information I had no clue about. In other words, if someone was stealing a little bit of money from me, imagine what kind of money they were taking from the big acts. So it was back to the locals in D.C. and back to my old life, which included the drug scene.

GOING BACK

Uptown had not changed one bit. Folks were still doing the same old thing. People were looking for fights, stealing from each other, getting high, taking, conning, you name it. I watched one of my get high friends, Lee Count get pistol whipped by one of the drug dealers in the neighborhood. It wouldn't have been so bad had they not grown up together. The dealer told Lee Count that if he ever came up short again with his money, he would kill him. Everybody knew that statement rang a lot of truth. One of the guys that I use to hang out with was found dead in his house shot between the eyes.

Another guy couldn't and wouldn't come outside for fear of his life, simply because he messed up a $50 bag of cocaine. It was time for me to move on. Way too much was happening uptown and since I didn't live up there anymore, there was no need for me to subject myself to that type of violence. I ventured in another section of the city where I knew other people.

Poochie was watching Jasmin for me most of the time. After hanging out and sometimes not coming home for days at a time, she got tired of my lifestyle and told me I couldn't come back to her place. I had not paid her rent for almost 2 months. Jerry told her that I needed to learn a lesson in order to get off drugs and to throw me out on the streets. Poochie needed the money and in addition to being tired of me told me I had to leave - and to take Jasmin with me.

I went to Capitol Hill at a gay friend of mine named Maurice. It was also a new experience for me because the people in NE were different from the people uptown, but nevertheless, still a drug scene. Maurice, Maurice's mother, his brother, his sister Paula and her 2 children were living in his one bedroom apartment. Since I use to go there to get high sometimes I was familiar with the surroundings. He said we could stay. His mother had 2 beds in her room where she, Paula and the 2 kids slept together. Steve, Maurice's brother, slept on the small bed. Maurice slept in the living room on the couch. Jasmin and I slept on the floor.

Why I even dealt with Maurice and his family is a question I still ask myself sometimes. I'm sure it had something to do with my situation at the time. You'll understand when I explain a little further in the book. His place was the only place I could think of to go at that time in that moment.

I'm thankful that he allowed us to come there, but I went to Hell and back in that apartment.

Like I said, there are many horrible and uncomfortable incidents that happened while I was in the streets smoking coke. Some are unforgettable; some I try not to think about and there are some incidents completely blacked out. Although what I am about to share with you may not seem like a big deal, it has always stayed with me.

I was smoking coke, and as usual, I spent every dollar, quarter, dime and penny I had. It was not uncommon to take the last bit of money and pool it together with other pipe heads in hopes of getting one more hit. Always one more hit.

Although there were 5 adults in Maurice's house, there had basically been no food in the house for a few days. Nobody had any money to buy any either.

Jasmin kept saying she was hungry and each time she did, it pierced my heart because there was no food there to feed her. I was tearing my brain apart trying to figure out what to do. In the 80s, there were no shelters or food banks you could go to.

I started making phone calls to people hoping I could borrow a few dollars to buy food but I had already exhausted most of my favors. My family and friends knew I got high and assumed me saying I needed money to buy food may have been a trick to get money.

In the meantime, Paula's kids were hungry too. She went to the store and stole some noodles and sausages. Although I was hungry as well, my focus was getting something for Jasmin. The aroma from the sausages forced me to ask Paula if Jasmin could get some of her food. She held her head down like there was something to think about, looked around the kitchen while stirring and made her decision. "There is only enough for my 2 girls. If I can steal for them, you can steal for yours."

She filled 2 bowls to the tip top which was obviously too much for them but she was determined not to have any left over. When the girls were full from eating, obviously not being able to eat the overfull bowls they were given, they took the rest of what they had and poured it in the trashcan, looked at me and laughed.

I recognize that Paula was not responsible for feeding my child but I know that had the shoe been on the other foot, I would have gladly shared.

I called Chubby, who came over and took me to the store to shop for groceries. I never forgot what Chubby did for me that day. I fed Jasmin a healthy meal and put the rest of the food away. By the next morning, all of the groceries were gone. Paula and her family devoured everything in the refrigerator without asking. I knew I had to get out of that house.

I need to move ahead just a bit to tell you this story so I'm going back to the Whitey Houston tour so that you will know what happened. The drug world, as many of you may know, has some pretty rough people. The right price would easily pay for a crime. You could almost hire a hit man, a murderer.

I came home one night while on tour with Whitney without anyone knowing I was coming, except Maurice. I told him that I was coming to town and asked if he could pick me up at the airport and not to let anyone know that I was coming. If he kept it quiet, I assured him the biggest cocaine party he could imagine. Maurice was gay so there was no need to worry about him wanting to have sex with me or any of the stupid stuff that comes with getting high with some guys. What he didn't know was that I had a total of $10,000 in cash on me, payment from my last week's work, but nobody knew it. Nobody.

I took out $1,000 as money to spend while I was home. The $9,000 was well hidden on me and was going in the bank the next day. Maurice picked me up at the airport as planned and took me to a pipe store to buy paraphernalia we needed for our cocaine party. It was a pain to have wait for a pipe to cool off once used so I bought 3 pipes. This way, we would not have to wait on one another's pipe to cool to take the next hit. I stopped in a drug area, completely unafraid. I had grown accustomed to those types of neighborhoods.

Any other time I would have gone to purchase the coke myself but I had the thought of the $9,000 in the back of my mind and was a little fearful of something going dead wrong and me having to give up that money. I gave Maurice $200 to purchase the cocaine. I didn't want to spend too much because I wanted to be sure what we were buying was good product.

We went to Maurice's apartment and got started, just the two of us. About a half hour into our party he told me his lover Brad was just getting out of school and was coming over. I was glad Brad came because when it was time to repurchase Maurice was too paranoid to go out in the street alone so Brad went with him.

On the way back, Maurice bought a guy with him, who had a girl with him, neither of whom I had ever seen before. Maurice claimed the guy wanted to go in half with me on some coke. I found this strange because I made it clear in the beginning that no one was to know I was there. Besides, I didn't need anyone to go in half with me because I had money. "What's up with that?" I thought.

Aside from me not knowing who the new guy and girl were, they both looked like cold-blooded killers. His mouth looked a little twisted and his eyes looked sneaky, dashing back and forth. He was always looking behind him like someone was following him.

She looked greasy, as if she hadn't had a shower for days. Her hair was supposedly pulled back in a ponytail but it was too short to really make one. She was skinny and talked real slick like each word was being sung. She did everything she could to act friendly. Chills ran up my back. I already knew I couldn't continue to get high around these two.

They sensed I didn't want them there but asked if it was okay if they took a hit. No sooner than they got settled to take the hit, in walks Paula. Now, remember, there were supposed to be only 2 people in that apartment, me and Maurice. Brad, Paula and 2 people I had never seen a day before in my life joined us.

Six Hundred Dollars is a lot of money in the hood. Being broke with a shot at a free $600 is like a dream come true in that environment. If the person who has the money is getting high with you, that's perfect if you plan to rob them. None of them knew I had the $9,000 on me because had they known that valuable information, I am sure they would have walked in the door and immediately put a bullet in my head and left me somewhere outside for dead.

Maurice and Paula made sure all three pipes were set up. I believe they wanted me to have just taken a hit by the time the plan went into action. I saw the gun on the floor under the table. The strange guy passed the gun with his foot to the strange girl. It was probably going to be a quick robbery but I was fortunately ahead of the game.

I knew in order to escape I had to leave my bags and purse in the living room. I quickly went over my "to do" steps in my head. I had to make sure I didn't pull too hard while taking the hit because I didn't want to become immobile. Cocaine will do that to you.

I got up after the hit and explained I needed some air. They fell for it, but watched to see if I was heading for my bags.

"I'm going out front to get some air. Be right back."

When I got out, I ran as fast as I could for fear they were behind me. Even though it was dark outside, I saw a cab at the end of the block waiting for the light. I waved my hands like a crazy woman and hailed the cab. He waited. I told the cab driver to take me to Maryland with no stops. I thought to myself as I went over the series of events that just took place that I must be out of my mind. It's a good thing I saw the gun with my own eyes; otherwise, I might not be here to tell you this story today.

I got to my destination, down from my high and called Maurice.

"I know what you and your crew were up to."

"Bunny what happened? You are geeking. I feel bad that you think something like that. I would never try to have your robbed."

About a month later, the same 2 people that Maurice and Paula bought in the apartment that I never saw were arrested for robbing a woman uptown, after almost beating her to death. Maurice and Paula knew those 2 people well.

Several months later, Maurice died from complications due to AIDS. Brad died about 2 weeks after Maurice. Paula's mother died shortly thereafter and from what I understand, Paula went to a drug rehab and is still struggling, but trying. I wish her well.

CURTIS

There were 2 guys that came to Maurice's house to cook drugs. Curtis and his friend were the new small time drug boys on the block. Curtis, clearly the one in charge, had a certain charisma about himself. He was quiet, gangsta and moved slow. On the streets they called him John Wayne. He was about 6'3" tall and skinny. Brown skinned, he wore a patch over his hand. Apparently he had a bad accident when he was a kid and since it was freezing outside the cold had an effect it. He kind of reminded me of a pirate. His voice was slow and deep and his eyes were so big they took a moment to research his surroundings. You couldn't really see his hair because he always wore a hood. He walked with his head leaned to the right with a slight pimp. His moustache was thick and dark and he was sporting a slight beard. I wasn't sure if I liked him or not because he looked too gangsta. I must admit he had street charm.

Once inside preparing his package, he gave everybody a piece of his cocaine, except me. Maurice got a piece because it was his apartment, Paula got a piece because she was Maurice's sister, Sheila, the person who introduced Maurice to Curtis was Curtis' friend so she got a piece. I was nobody. I had no connection. When I asked for a hit, he got up and left, claiming he hated leeches.

I saw Curtis often out on the corners of northeast Washington, near 7th & G Streets, NE, several blocks away from the Rayful Edmond crew trying to sell coke. (Rayful Edmond was notorious in the drug world and is now serving life without a possible parole. His arrest was one of the largest busts in the history of the drug world.) Curtis was conveniently located in the area so a lot of the locals purchased from him. Curtis made no money because he smoked his own product.

One evening, one of my buddies and I wanted to smoke but all of the drug smoking spots were unavailable. Curtis suggested we use his spot. Although he was usually distant and mean, he took us to an apartment not too far from where they sold drugs. He had keys to this guy Tony's apartment. I thought Tony was too nice to be dealing with people like Curtis who took full control of the apartment, as if it was his. Tony didn't breathe one word, probably because he was one of those really kind, sweet Gay guys. We must have stayed there for about a half hour and left.

I started seeing Curtis around the neighborhood, a different person. We'd talk sometimes and I would hang out with him on the streets some evenings when I didn't have to work the next day.

Even though I was only hanging out with Curtis, people considered us a couple.

He treated me like a queen and kept me laughing. He was always trying to think of something to do for me. However, all of his money went to drugs just like mine. Every time I got paid, I always took out enough to give to Poochie, who was back to watching Jasmin a good bit of the time. I had to make sure Jasmin had everything she needed.

If I didn't take money out up front, Jasmin would have suffered the consequences. I was not putting myself in a situation with no food because of my past experiences even though most people who smoked coke didn't care one thing about food while getting high. It was after you were done getting high that you felt the effects.

The first time I met Deena, Curtis' mother, I noticed she was sassy and fly with a drink in one hand and a cigarette in the other. One morning, around 6:00 a.m. Deena walked up as I was knocking on her door, hoping Curtis would quickly come down before she cursed me out for knocking on her door that time of morning. She had been out gambling at a card game all night and didn't fuss at all about me being there. She looked like she could be Curtis' sister because of her youthful look. Speaking of sisters, Curtis had a little sister who was about 8 or 9 at the time, born to Deena and her late husband. He also had a sister a year older than him, born to Deena and her first husband who was Curtis' father too, another sister in between Curtis and the baby sister, born to Curtis' father and his current wife, an older stepsister from his mother's husband and his German girlfriend and a stepbrother, from Curtis' stepmother (his father's wife) and her first husband. There was a lot of drama in that family, but who am I to talk? There was a lot of drama in my family too.

Deena's deceased husband bought her a house on Capitol Hill before he died at a time when Capitol Hill was occupied by the Black community. She was a shrewd businesswoman and knew how to get what she wanted. One of the things she wanted was a girlfriend for Curtis. She was delighted to see me and took account of my looks and size and before I knew it, put together a wardrobe of some of the finest clothes she either could no longer wear or no longer wanted. Most of them were size 4 with a couple of 2's and 1's. I could fit almost everything except a few of the 4's that were a little large on me. Deena was hoping that I was the woman to take Curtis off her hands and out of her house. We got along well in the beginning - and the end. In between was another story.

Curtis and I rented the top floor at Deena's but didn't stay long. We moved across the street with a woman who had a lot of drug activity going on. She allowed some big drug boys from Jamaica to set up shop on the top floor of her house, and that is when things started spiraling out of control. The sad part is, like me, she was really not exposed to the street, per se and had no clear idea of how to run a drug house. The house got busted. We were forced to move out.

We spent some time with one of his old school friends on the other side of town. The friend, Billy, looked just like Tony, the guy whose apartment Curtis had keys to when I first met him. They could have almost passed for brothers. Billy was a pretty boy. Dark straight hair and light skinned with dark features. He was short, small and talked all the time. He always tried to be hard but he was a really feminine guy.

We stayed with Billy for a couple of weeks. They were doing drugs in that house too but not as bad as where we left. I found a one bedroom apartment around the corner from where he lived, the first place I had since I sold the house Jasmin and I lived in. It felt good to be back in my own place, but I was still getting high almost every day.

The avenue was a haven for purchasing drugs. They sold all kinds of junk. You might buy a peanut and not know until you got home. You couldn't test it on the street and you had to be extremely careful for fear of the police. I worked hard on my temp assignments and extra hard on the weekends in nightclubs. To get beat out of it was not only frustrating but heart wrenching because there was no way to get that money back.

I was almost 6 years into doing drugs, living the horrible life of working for the drug man. I just barely paid the bills because most of the money went to the pipe. I had a couch to sit or lay on in the living room, a dining room set and a bed and a set of bunk beds. I had to creep to get high because Jasmin was home and Poochie's kids, Scoobie and Cashana were with me. One of Poochie's twin stepsons, Eric, was diagnosed with Leukemia. Poochie and her husband Sam, the twins' father, were spending a great deal of time at the hospital and kept Eric's twin brother, Derrick, nearby. I didn't mind keeping her kids considering she had always helped me with Jasmin.

One morning, after getting high all night, I woke up in a bent position, unable to stand straight. I was in excruciating pain and could just barely walk. Curtis took one look at me and rushed me to the emergency room where I was tested for 2 days. The hospital couldn't find anything wrong with me. I was furious because the doctors gave me Motrin and told me there was nothing else they could do. They had run every test possible and hopefully, whatever pain I was experiencing, would go away. I went home still bent over.

I prayed about my condition. I was tired of living that lifestyle and more tired that I was not able to offer Jasmin a better life. She didn't deserve this. I was tired of being tired, staying up late at night getting high and going to work exhausted. I was tired of always explaining why I looked so bad, tired of explaining that I weighed 99 pounds because of my thyroid knowing it was the drugs. I was tired of lying about everything because of the drug world. I remember walking past a guy in a 7-Eleven and without even looking at me good he said "excuse me dude." *He didn't even know I was a woman.* Another guy pointed me out to his friend and said "man, look at her. She looks like a stick." I felt humiliated. What happened to the cutie pie that guys use to admire? What happened to me? Why couldn't I just quit? Why?

I started thinking about how I ruined my life in the drug world. There was no life there. The only place you could and would eventually end up would be dead. There was no future whatsoever in that world. I started praying. That was all I could do and I knew in my soul that the only way I would get help is if I asked God himself to help me. Otherwise I was at a dead end and may as well give up. I needed hope and a blessing.

I prayed harder than I ever prayed before in my life because I wanted God to hear me and hear me good. I begged for His mercy and asked him to please deliver me from the evil at hand. I did the unthinkable. I made a deal. With God.

In the past, I never made any deals with God because I knew that there was a possibility that I could go back on my word so I never included the Lord. But this was different. I was sick of the life I was living. If He delivered me from my sickness, I would never smoke another drop of cocaine as long as I lived. I reached deep down in my soul with prayer. I was tired of the drug scene and scared of God.

On January 1, 1990, after coming home from the hospital, I went to sleep - woke up and stood straight up.

A couple of our friends were knocking at the door with a New Years gift. They had an 8-ball (8 oz.) of cocaine and wanted to share it with me and Curtis. They threw it on the table and told us to help ourselves. I just looked at them. The devil was busy. I told them I couldn't smoke any of it because of the deal I made with God. Curtis looked at me like I was crazy and said he didn't make any promises and hand him the pipe.

The three of them proceeded to smoke the coke. I stood there the whole while and watched. I was waiting to see my reaction. Would I be able to hold out? Would the drug over power me? Should I leave out for fear of giving in? Should I go in another room and close the door? I mean, for cryin' out loud. I made a deal with God! I was almost in tears that my desire was not there, happy about it and wanted to scream at those drugs that they meant nothing and were nothing to me! I was determined to sit there and watch to see if I could do it. With each scream that came with the smoke in the air, it meant absolutely nothing to me. When all of the coke was gone, I knew I was going to be okay. I was through with that drug. Healed, spared, delivered and saved.

PEACE

After a while people could see I didn't do drugs anymore. I gained weight, my skin changed, attitude changed and I was able to save money. I didn't go to any rehabs, nor seek any help from anybody because I believed God delivered me and that was good enough for me. Curtis told me that I would be back. Nobody could just quit like I did, nobody.

About 6 months later I told Curtis he should really think about giving up drugs. He was coming in late in the evenings, constantly back and forth up the avenue and asked me for money whenever and however he could. After a while his asking for money got to be old.

It got so that all of his money went to drugs while I paid all of the bills. He was bringing people in and out of the house at any given hour and also allowed people to knock on our door any time of the day or night. After not getting any rest for a few days, I sat him down and told him we had to do something. I gave him 6 months to straighten up or I was leaving. I started working for a major law firm and couldn't continue on with the lifestyle I was in because I wanted better. He said he would. He didn't.

I waited the 6 months, found another apartment, told Curtis to stay in the one he was in and I was moving out. He was not happy about that because it meant that he would have to be responsible for his actions and his bills.

I found peace when I moved out of the apartment. People were not running back and forth or in and out of the apartment and no one knocked on my door. There was no one but me and Jasmin. She loved it with just the two of us.

Several months later, he moved in with another girl. He gained weight, was clean cut and going to church every Sunday. He said the new girl helped him realize he needed to get off drugs and he did. It had been months since he did any drugs or drank any liquor, so he said. I was happy for him and wished him well.

"You still perform at the Ibex cuz I want to bring my friend to see you."

I told him I had not been there since we split, but I was thinking about it and would let him know. I can't believe I was a little jealous.

THE MARRIAGE AND THE BABY

We kept running back and forth into each other and eventually got back together. We must have stayed together for several months when he asked me to marry him. We were both doing well and having a lot of fun enjoying each other's company. I said yes and we got married in Upper Marlboro, Maryland in front of a justice of the peace on his birthday. He said if we married on his birthday, which was July 3, he would never forget our anniversary.

On my birthday of that year, December 14, 1991, I learned that I was pregnant. I don't know how that happened, considering I was told that I would never have any more children.

I also didn't get a response to the letter I sent to Larry reminding him of Jasmin's birthday. There was a little gnaw in the back of my mind that reminded me that he had to remember her birthday. Her birthday was December 12, his was December 13 and mine was December 14.

Curtis couldn't and would not believe that I was pregnant until he saw the actual sonogram simply because he knew of the treatment I had earlier for my thyroid. He was excited and was hoping for a boy. There we go with that boy stuff again.

Approximately 2 months into the pregnancy the baby was trying to abort itself. The doctor recommended a drug that had not been approved by the Food and Drug Administration but wanted to know if I was willing to try it to save this new little person's life. What the drug would do was build a bed for the baby to secure its position. I was forced on bed rest and told it was important to follow all of the doctor's orders in order for the baby to possibly make it. I was willing to do and try whatever it took to save this baby's life because I was already attached to it.

I told my doctor about my experience while delivering Jasmin. That couldn't happen again. That type of delivery at my age with the new baby would kill me, or so I told myself.

My doctor assured me that this was not 1979 but 1992 and if a woman didn't want to deliver naturally, they were compelled to give pain medicine or something similar to help with delivery. I asked her if she could put that in writing. She said no, but promised I would not suffer.

The baby was due on August 13, 1992 but the pains started on August 6. These pains were not as intense in the beginning as they were with Jasmin. They were mild and I was able to get a shower before going to the hospital, which was about 1:00 a.m. I woke up the entire apartment. Fear immediately set in and I told Jasmin and Cashana that this was not a time for joking and that the baby was ready. Curtis drove us all to George Washington University Hospital where I was admitted immediately. The first thing that came out of my mouth was the fact that my doctor promised I would not have to suffer. The staff assured me I would not.

The pains grew intense with each 5 or 10 minutes until I was almost at an unbearable stage. My doctor had not been in my room the entire night. I was getting nervous because the staff was not administering any drugs for pain and my breathing was becoming labored. They lied. They were going to let me suffer through this delivery and the tears started. I was in pain and the moaning didn't help the pain at all. I was delirious.

When my doctor came in, she immediately ordered pain medication which included an epidural. Thank God. I again thought about my mother. She went through this six times. I know that some women have it easier than others, but if Ma went through that many times, I can not imagine her taking any crap off anybody. Child bearing, in my opinion, is serious.

After all I went through the baby girl was delivered by c-section. Curtis and I couldn't spell some of the names mothers were giving their kids because we couldn't spell any of the eishas or juans or itas. We named her Michelle after one of Curtis' cousins in New York. He was one proud father and almost would not let anyone hold her. He gave her to me.

I looked at this beautiful baby and thought of Jasmin. This new baby lit my heart up again. I started crying. I welcomed her into the world. It was as though she looked at me and said thank you but it was me, in my heart that said thank you to her. She blessed me by coming and I was happy that morning. Having Curtis there with me made me understand how blessed I was because thinking back to when I had Jasmin made me sad all over, but this was a time for rejoicing so I put the sadness out and watched my new baby with excitement. I looked up and thanked God once again.

We went home with our little new person who changed the whole household. There were bottles to be made, diapers to change, baths to give and prayers to say. After all, Michelle had a hard time getting here but the drug worked and she was born healthy.

Curtis was phenomenal with the whole scene of a new baby. He made her bottles everyday, changed her religiously, played with her and adored her with everything he had. He should have received some kind of best dad award.

A new baby meant we would have to find a house to live in - the apartment was too small. We found a nice old house in NE Washington and moved that March. Because the house was old and there was so much to do, we were always at work. Michelle needed constant attention and we were all busy doing our share of trying to keep the house up.

Curtis wanted to know how I felt about him getting a Doberman Pinscher? I grew up with dogs and they are just like babies. Dogs need a lot of attention that we didn't have at that time. Maybe after Michelle grew up a little, we could get her a dog. In addition to that, dogs could be expensive. He actually wanted 2. There was no way we were going to get dogs at that time.

He got the dogs anyway. They weren't small puppies. They were about 6 months old, almost grown. They came in playful and active. I was angry because the dogs were too special to stay outside. Someone would try to steal them before the night was over. Curtis said they were good protection until that first big poop. I had just changed Michelle and couldn't understand why it still smelled so bad. It never occurred to me that it was one of the dogs until I saw the pile. It was so big and awful I thought a gorilla had been there. The pile was stinking and had to be removed and guess who had to do it?

Curtis came home and heard the story and my mouth. He assured me that he would train them in record time. Yeah right.

Not only were the dogs pooping and urinating all over the place, they had not been walked at all. I also noticed that the couch and a pair of my expensive heels had been chewed up and torn apart. Having just come home from work, picking up Michelle, tired, exhausted and needing to do my regular chores, there I was with urine and poop everywhere, torn up shoes, clothes here and there and a sight of furniture slowly but surely deteriorating. I was not happy. The dogs needed to be fed and walked. Where was Curtis? By this time, although I was fed up, I looked in the little doggy faces and realized I had developed affection for them, but I was still angry.

After seeing how disturbed I was Curtis decided to build a dog house outside in the backyard until he was able to train them. He had no job and told me the cost to buy the wood and parts to build the house for both dogs. I complained again that I had just paid $200 for parking tickets he got which were originally $100 but since he never told me about the tickets, they doubled. I weighed the facts - a couple of dog houses and get the dogs out of my hair or no dog houses and continue to clean poop, urine and trash.

The wood houses looked like 2 pieces of junk. One good rain and wind and that was the end of that - they would go down for sure -- and that's exactly what happened. He decided he would get 2 new fiberglass state of the art dog houses he saw for sale. That would also allow the dogs to stay outside in the winter. The dogs were still not trained to poop outside, nor were they being walked by anyone but me.

The expensive fiberglass houses proved to be unworthy of their value because the dogs bit right through them effortlessly. Between the dog houses, equipment, food and cleansing materials, the dogs were pretty expensive. It got so it was like having 3 babies instead of one. Curtis was rarely home. As usual, he was across town with his friends and his new thing - Remy Martin - VSOP.

We'd only been married for about 2 years when he came home one night with huge glassy eyes. I knew that look all too well. I had to ask him.

"Are you okay?"

"Yeah I'm okay. Why wouldn't I be? Shit, I'm fine; you the one I should be asking if they okay. A motha fucka can't come home wif out a lotta questions. Shit is sickening. I had a couple of beers and a drink here and there and the first thing come to your mind is I been smokin".

I didn't want to believe it but he had been smoking crack. I didn't have to wonder if it was true, I knew it.

"If I wanna smoke, I'ma smoke and that's that. I don't need anybody asking me a lot of questions. Do I ask you a lot of questions when you running up to Atlantic City? Naw, I let you go. All you do is go to work and come home and act like you done did something. I do everything around this mo' fck'r. I'm tired of yo' shit. Every time I ask you for a dollar you act like you ain't got it or somethin'."

This went on for a while and I listened to him; made a few comments and got my ear's worth so I decided to go to bed to try to get some sleep, concerned because I had been around him enough to know when he was high and when he wasn't. No question about it he was high and changing for the worse.

Working in his father's flower shop was not enough. He needed a real job with real benefits. FedEx was hiring. He got the job driving a Fed Ex Truck - part time.

We lived about 3 minutes from the Fed Ex offices so I couldn't understand why he got up at 3:00 am not having to be at work until 6:30 am.

He called people on the phone, talked loud, cooked all kinds of breakfast and lunch food for his meals. Every morning he would wake me completely out of my sleep. I talked to him about getting himself ready at night but that didn't sit well with him.

If I was exhausted and didn't hear him, he would wake me up out of my sleep for the smallest things - have you seen my other sock? Where did you put my other shirt? Did you move my keys? Did you buy some bread yesterday? Did you turn the light out in the basement last night? Anything to have me up. Almost every day I went to work dragging.

I decided to sleep in Michelle's room at night but that was worse. The big glassy eyes, the alcohol, cigarettes and drugs were already taking its toll on me and paranoia was settling in. He said I was part of the FBI.

He was spending money quicker than we could make it. He started borrowing money from me and not really paying the household back.

One instance, after he spent all of his money and a good portion of mine, he asked me for more.

"I don't have any more money."

"You're a lying bitch, bitch."

The words stunned me for a moment and I could only look at him. Not only had he never addressed me in that manner, no one had. I had to ask him to repeat what he said because I couldn't believe him.

"What did you say?"

"You heard what I said."

We argued back and forth over the fact that I didn't have any money all night. I felt my blood rising as a result of the screaming and felt like I was about to have a heart attack. I stopped talking altogether and let him duke it out all on this own, all night long. It was the first time I ever saw anyone foam at the mouth. When I think about it, I can truly say that of all of the verbal abuse, all of the mental anguish and the emotional stress that I encountered, watching that man foam at his mouth had to be the worse. Can you imagine the number of bitches, m'fers, kiss my asses, f'ck yous, suck my so n' so's, lick my this, you rotten mf'er, etc. he had to say in order for his saliva to thicken into what appeared to look like a small piece of cotton coming out of his mouth? I cringed every time I saw it and felt bad for him. I knew that drugs were playing an important role in this action, nevertheless it was devastating.

The next morning I was exhausted, again. He followed me around the house still arguing about money until I was ready to leave and glad. I couldn't take the rant and rave any more.

I opened the door to leave. He took his foot, shoved my behind pushing me out the door. He immediately locked the door. I stopped with intentions of going back to ask him why but I didn't have it in me.

There's no way I could continue with that life style. It was like back in the old days. He was doing drugs full time, spending all the money he had and any he could find. He was out of control and the arguing back and forth was getting to me. We needed to go our separate ways.

He took one look at me and said "You ain't going nowhere and neither am I." Deep down inside, he knew I was serious. He also knew that I couldn't just jump up and leave that day or that week. It would take time for me to find a place.

He asked if it would be okay if his nephew, Grady, whose woman had just put him out, stayed with us. He said as payment Grady could help him around the house. That was the first time I heard of this nephew. After meeting Grady, I noticed that he seemed to display feminine traits, like constantly putting his hands on his hips while talking, pointing his finger at you and talking in that high pitched voice with a controlled lisp. Most guys I knew didn't say things to another guy like "Hey Boo Boo. I like those slacks" whit emphasis on the "like." I let that thought go once Curtis said that Grady had kids and of course a wife.

Grady stayed with us a while and Curtis spent a lot of time in the basement with him, getting high, or at least that is what I was thinking. Grady never went to see this woman or his kids so it seemed a little strange to me that he had this so-called relationship. When I questioned Curtis about it again, it seemed as if he got nervous. He told Grady he had to move.

Not long after Grady was gone, Curtis asked if a guy named Mark could stay with us. Mark was homeless but got a check every month from SSI and would be more than happy to help Curtis around the house.

I not only detected a serious feminine side in Mark but he got high too. When Mark talked, he sounded exactly like a woman. Curtis assured me that it was all in my mind because according to him, Mark was a womanizer. I couldn't figure that out considering Mark never talked about women, much less going to visit one. I smelled a rat.

HIV/AIDS

In the 1980s and 90s, the conversation on HIV/AIDS could cause verbal and physical violence in some neighborhoods. People spoke about what they would do to someone who gave them AIDS. It was anywhere from beating to killing them especially since the attitude was I'm going to die anyway. To be given an AIDS diagnosis was the same as getting a death sentence, which was right around the corner. No one wanted any association with a person who had the disease. Dying from AIDS could be horrible. Some people went blind or lost mobile skills. Some were ridden with sores and infections. Some suffered unbearably. Some cried uncontrollably when dealt the news. Others lost it and most of the time needed mental therapy. Some did drugs and alcohol to try to "high" it away.

AIDS was rampaging through neighborhoods. You heard daily how someone died from complications due to the disease. From next door neighbor to movie star, AIDS had no boundaries and anyone could become victim. For a while, many Black women were contracting the disease in record numbers because Black men were secretly having sex with men and then giving it, unsuspected, to their women.

Curtis saw how unhappy I was about being with him and knew that I was serious about leaving. July 16, 1998, he nonchalantly walked in the bedroom and told me there was something he had to tell me. I figured he was going to say something about drug money he owed someone and if he didn't pay them he was going to have to fight, move or hide. I never in a million years expected him to say what he was about to say. Nor was I ready for it.

When he told me this, he was not sad, scared, frightened or anything. He just said it with no emotion. He sat down on the bed without so much as even looking at me and delivered his message. He went to DC General's Venereal Disease Clinic because he took an HIV test.

"My test came back positive. You need to be tested."

I just looked at him. A frown covered my face. I was shocked. Spellbound by the nightmare in the words he spoke; unable to understand any of what he had just said. Did he say HIV test? HIV as in AIDS? Did he say he took a test? Was he talking to me? He couldn't be serious. Did he just say death? He was looking at me waiting for a response.

"I'm HIV positive and you need to be tested because you might be HIV positive too."

Was he serious? I had to ask him to repeat it. I couldn't believe what I was hearing. How many times had all of us in both our families talked about this very thing?

"What did you say Curtis? What did you say?"

"You heard me. I'm positive and you need to be tested."

In the center of my head the words "if he has it, so do you" were slamming themselves in my brain like they were smacking me. Oh God! No! No! No! This can't be true, please say it's not true God. Please. I didn't do anything to deserve this!

My ears were ringing and my head was spinning. I couldn't take my eyes off him. I was weak and almost sick. This had to be a bad joke gone wrong. My chest felt like it was caving in. Was I getting ready to fall out? Should I grab the wall? I wanted to scream and felt like I couldn't breathe.

I started shaking my head no. He was lying. Liar. Just trying to get me upset. That's what he was doing. Yeah. That's what it was. Just a lying dog. Had to be. Lately he was always saying mean nasty things trying to depress and hurt me. No way could he do to me what he was trying to do. This was another one of his sick tricks. But, wait a minute, he said he had been tested and was positive? All of the words I was thinking started running after each other. AIDS? HIV? SICK? BLIND? DEATH? No way could this be true. It felt like I was in a trance because I could almost not move.

Why did he hate me so much? What had I done for him to try to trick me by telling me this lie? Was he trying to make me angry, sad, scared and hurt? What was he looking for by sharing this sick trick? It had to be a mistake. Wasn't it? We had been married too long for him to be HIV positive, unless, wait a minute! Unless he had been cheating! Jesus Christ. I thought to myself what about Michelle? Does she have it? Oh God no! And poor Jasmin. Her family would be wiped out because I knew that if Curtis had it, so did I and more than likely, Michelle.

I had to lie down and couldn't get out of bed for 2 days. I was weak and felt like I couldn't breathe. It felt like a hole was in my chest. My head was light, my legs like jelly and this man who had been treating me like a piece of dirt just announced his death sentence and possibly mine and Michelle's. I kept wondering if he already knew about this. I was angry and not sure which way to turn or what to believe. But suppose he had it all this time and didn't know he had it? Would that put him in a different category? I felt confused, rejected, angry and upset. I wanted to tell him to get out right then and there but I knew he would never leave without force.

Then I started feeling sorry for him but angry at the same time. And it hit me! Curtis wore condoms almost the whole time we were married! Maybe I didn't have it. I tried to calculate the number of times we had unprotected sex. The question of why a married man would wear condoms came to mind again.

A long time ago Curtis came up with an ugly infection he claimed he got as a result of having unprotected sex with me. When I say ugly, I mean ugly. His private area was full of red bumps layered on top of a big beige rash that looked like some kind of eerie fish from the bottom of the ocean. I didn't have the rash but went to see my doctor anyway. Nothing was found. Curtis continued to wear condoms claiming if he didn't wear them, the infections came back. My gut feeling told me that he knew about his condition already.

I became so overwhelmed with this disclosure that I couldn't sleep, work, eat, socialize or barely talk. I was depressed and determined not to get tested. If I was going to die, I didn't want to know. I wanted to be alone.

I was scared. Numb. I didn't want to talk to him because this was just plain wrong. How could he do this?

Curtis forbade me to tell his family or anyone. This was the most devastating secret I could ever imagine trying to keep. I needed an outlet so I sought professional therapy.

Where I grew up seeing a therapist automatically meant that you were coo coo. Many people in the Black community didn't understand. If you went, it was usually a well-kept secret.

I didn't care. I attended the first session with the therapist alone because Curtis simply would not go, then and it would be a while before he would go to one meeting. Those first 45 minutes I must have cried the whole time. Just the thought of dying from that dreadful disease devastated me.

"You must get tested immediately. You owe that to your children. Besides, Sylvia, you need to get as much education as you can about this so that you can understand what is happening to you and your family. Education is key."

I took her advice and learned as much as I could. In my community people believed that AIDS laid dormant for years but what they didn't understand is that was true, IF you didn't get tested.

I started ordering information and packets from different organizations and was online daily to read about HIV. I found information on some web sites that emotionally helped me and some that devastated me.

I made the decision to get tested. It was almost like a relief. Curtis went with me and wanted to retest himself to confirm from a private doctor whether or not he was in fact, infected. A quick thought raced through my mind as to why he would go to a clinic in the first place anyway. Why didn't he go to the private doctor in the beginning?

The doctor said it would take 3 business days before the results came back and since it was a Thursday I would not know until that Tuesday. It was the longest weekend of my life.

I convinced Curtis that we at least needed to tell his immediate family because if he died, they would hold me responsible and blame me for not allowing them to share his last days with them. He agreed.

I must have cried the whole weekend and prayed to God to please bless me. Please. I was sick with worry and couldn't talk to anyone because my mind was consumed with thoughts of having the disease. All I did was wait. Wait for a possible death sentence. Waiting to know if it was true. Waiting. Waiting. Waiting. I didn't sleep or eat.

I went to work that Monday and couldn't focus on anything. If you asked me to help you, I would tell you the time. If you asked me about phone calls I might tell you what time I got in.

I would receive the results of my test in the morning. I tossed and turned and stressed myself the entire night.

Tuesday morning. I must have watched the clock from 8:30 until 9:05 and finally called. The receptionist answered:

"Dr. Van Dam's office.

"Hi - This is Sylvia Morrison."

"Oh, your results came back negative."

Just like that. No let me check your records, no hold on for a moment, no give me one minute. She knew before I even called and was ready for me. I almost couldn't talk from shock or happiness. I wasn't sure.

"You mean my HIV test is negative?"

"Yes"

"Are you sure?"

"Yes. Would you like a copy?"

"Yes. What happens now?"

"You should probably speak with the doctor."

"What about my husband?" I was hoping and praying that maybe the clinic made a mistake.

"I'm sorry but I cannot give you that information. He will have to call for his own results."

"Ok. Thank you. Thank you so much."

I hung up the phone, looked at the base of the phone for a few seconds and then broke down and cried like a baby.

I called my doctor back to find out what I already knew. I would have to be tested again in 6 months and every 6 months thereafter if I was exposing myself to the disease, especially if I was having unprotected sex. He explained that it took about 6 months for the disease to show up in your system after exposure. Fortunately, I already knew that information because of what I read.

Curtis held his breath when I told him of my negative results. It was as if he was confused and didn't understand how I didn't have the disease. I could tell he was a little disturbed by his quiet demeanor and slow response. He wanted to be able to say that I gave it to him but if I didn't have it, how could I have given it to him?

The infectious disease doctor told Curtis that based on his viral load and his cd4 cell count he needed to start a cocktail regiment immediately. It consisted of 3 different sets of pills. If it didn't work, he would be placed on different regiments until they found a suitable match. It was important to eat well, no alcohol or drug use if he wanted to live a long and fruitful life. He also explained that people whose cd4 cell count fell below 200 had full blown AIDS.

On the way home we filled the prescriptions to start his medication that day. I was taken aback when I saw the first set of pills. If you look at your baby finger, the first line closest to the top on the pinky, measure from that line to the top, you will get an idea as to how big that one pill was. He had to take 6 of those. They had nothing to do with the 16 or so other pills he had to take. I broke down and cried, quietly thanking God for not allowing the disease in my body.

Curtis put all 6 pills and the others in his mouth at one time and got them down. Twenty minutes later he sick. I was still mentally dealing with where and how he got this disease. The medicine required that he eat whenever he could. He also should have eaten before the pills. I fixed him 2 sandwiches, a salad and tea and served him in bed. I was still mentally questioning how this happened and couldn't think of anything else. An hour or so after he ate, he said he was hungry again. I fixed him a couple more sandwiches, a bowl of soup and more tea.

An hour or 2 later, he was hungry again, to a point that it was growing out of control. I thought maybe he had a stomach worm because he ate like something was helping him to eat. I was tired of fixing sandwiches and soup and other food but each time I looked at him I felt sorry because the only thing that came to mind was that he was going to die. He knew that I was feeling that and took advantage.

"Get me something to eat. I'm hungry. Give me some more tea, where my chips? What's taking you so long?"

I felt he needed whatever he was asking for but all the while still thinking to myself, where did it come from? How did he get it? How long does he have to live?

After a day or so on the cocktail regiment, he got really sick. It must have been around 1:00 a.m. when he complained about his chest hurting. He was twisting and turning and started screaming.

"BUNNY! BUNNY! My heart! My heart!"

I had already dialed 911 when he started twisting uncontrollably. I thought that was it. He was dying. I calculated in my head that if he got this virus back in the 80's, death could be settling in on his life now.

The ambulance arrived and took him to the hospital. Michelle and I followed and there was no question as to admitting him because he was deathly sick. We were given permission to spend the night in his room. They IV'd his arm and had him hooked up to all kinds of medical contraptions and equipment. Fortunately, the next morning his condition calmed.

I was feeling sorry that he might die soon. I know that he had been evil to me but I felt in my heart that no one deserved to die from this horrid disease.

The team of doctors came in early that morning and told Curtis that he had a slight heart attack possibly as a result of his cocktail regiment. They would have to change his medication.

Later that morning while Curtis slept, I picked up his chart to see if I could figure out exactly what the doctors wrote. To my surprise, I learned that Curtis' cd4 cell count was 11. 11? I had to rethink what the infectious disease doctor said about the cd4 cell count. He said that if your count was under 200, the CDC noted that as having FULL BLOWN AIDS! Oh my God! He's got full blown AIDS! I felt my head getting light and my heart started racing. He is not only HIV positive, he is full blown AIDS. No wonder they let us spend the night. With a common cold, infected lungs and bad medicine he could have died. This meant, as far as I understood, we already lived through the HIV status and didn't know it. Or should I say I didn't know it?

Michelle and I stayed each night with him until he was released from the hospital with a new cocktail. He wasted no time getting back to his old ways. He rode to Mr. Taylor's and hooked up with a few of his get high buddies. He would be gone for days at a time. He missed work and didn't tell his job his condition. He went in when he felt like it.

Approximately 6 months after the first test, I went back to be tested again, not because I was having unprotected sex but because I knew that it took about that much time for the disease to actually show up in your system. When the doctor gave me the news I almost fainted. He told me that there's an enzyme in my blood that will not allow the AIDS virus to attach itself. More than likely, Michelle had the same enzyme. I just looked at him. Shocked. Happy. Tears. Disbelief!

"You're kidding right? Really?"

I will never in my lifetime be able to describe the joy or the incredible feeling I had when I heard those words. It was a blessing I would never be able to thank God enough for. I think I cried harder at that revelation than anything in my life.

"Thank you Lord. Thank you."

I was numb and, grateful. I must have sat there for half an hour thinking. Teary eyed. Head down. Hands clasped together. Overwhelmed. Thankful. When I told Curtis my news he became more of a nightmare. I understood his devastation IF he just found out. He was getting high in the house and kept me up almost every night.

One morning, I noticed my purse wide open. Curtis took my credit card in the middle of the night, hocking gas. What that means is, if you pulled up in the gas station, wanted $20 worth of gas, he would tell you to give him $10 in cash and he would pump $20 worth of gas in your car. It didn't register to me until I got a bill for over $900. He denied it.

He came in the bedroom one night with a gun wrapped in a towel. Through his paranoia he locked the door and hid behind it.

"I know you with the FBI. What did you tell 'em 'bout me?" pointing the gun at the ceiling as if someone was on top of our roof. In my mind today, if someone came around me in that state, I would do everything I could to get away as fast as I could because the look on that man's face was horrifying. Even I can't understand what made me stay in that house.

One day, I was so tired from being up a good part of the week listening to him argue and watching him foam at the mouth, I fell into a deep sleep. I woke up coughing uncontrollably. Michelle was coughing too. I opened my eyes and there he was, on his knees next to the bed, looking at me straight in the face, his face almost aligned with mine, coughing as well, and eyes big as silver dollars. In his hallucination, he thought I was trying to do something to him. I can't remember if it was mace or pepper spray he sprayed but we all had to get up in the middle of the night and stand outside. It was a real nightmare.

Another night he came in and asked for money. If I had any I would have gladly given it to him to get him out of the house and let me have some peace. He was determined I had some. When I couldn't produce any, I saw madness in his eyes. He screamed demanding my wedding rings. I handed them to him. He sold the rings for a $10 rock of crack.

Michelle, who was around 6 years old, was sad when she saw how upset I was about the rings. It must have had an impact on her as well because shortly after, we went on a trip to Atlantic City. With her allowance money she stopped in a little store on the Boardwalk and made a very special purchase. That night, in the hotel room, she sat me down.

"I have something for you."

When she gave it to me, I couldn't speak. Inside the most beautifully wrapped little, tiny, pretty box was a small band surrounded in diamonds. They were fake stones, but nevertheless, in her mind, a wedding ring surrounded with diamonds. I was stunned. When she announced what was on her mind, I couldn't move.

"Now you have your rings back."

She politely put on her pajamas and got in the bed, all while I was sitting there with my mouth open unable to say a word. She went to sleep, just like that. I must have cried about that the whole night. It was one of the single most special things anyone had ever done for me in my life.

There were nights he got the last money out of my purse while I slept not caring what would happen the next morning at the subway or the bus stop when it was time to pay my fare.

I put a stop to that by wearing my purse around my neck whenever I was home to prevent him from going in it.

MY CHANCE - I CAN GET OUT NOW

I prayed to God for an answer. Do I just up and leave, should I move out and move on? I can't take this anymore. Lord, I need a sign. So many different horrors happened during this time period.

Jasmin needed a ride to the airport to get back to college but Curtis said he needed to use the car. He and Jasmin were back and forth about who needed the car the most. His new thing was riding around looking for people who were trying to hail cabs for a lesser fee than a cab fare.

"It's my mother's car Curtis"

"I don't care whose car it is. I'll make it so that nobody can drive the car."

He opened the hood and took out one of the cables so that I couldn't start the car. I had to get a ride for Jasmin to get to the airport. And boy was I in for a surprise.

I never got sick at work and if I did, I would try to work through it. This particular day, I was sick and nauseous and called the house to have Curtis pick me up since I couldn't drive the car. There was no answer. I paged him - no answer.

I caught a cab home. The car was not in front of the house and I figured since he never answered the phone, he wasn't there. I got the mail and went inside. While sorting the mail, I heard laughter coming from the bedroom area and wondered if someone was in the house. But of course no one was there because Curtis wasn't home, so I thought.

It was strange hearing the voices and the laughter. Where was it coming from? It started sounding like it was right in the house. I put the mail down, listened carefully and walked towards the bedroom. When I turned into the doorway of the bedroom, there they were. Curtis and some street woman were there naked having a "party."

He was standing there looking at me in shock. Butter ball naked. The woman was sitting on the comforter on my bed with a bare bottom. She obviously had not been to the bathroom so I am sure the juices were flowing on my bed from her booty. I was steaming.

My initial reaction was to kill him. I could get away with it! But then I thought about it. He just wasn't worth it.

I picked up the phone and called the police so that I could get off my mind doing anything stupid. As I was on the phone, Terry, Curtis' friend walked in from purchasing drugs. He was the reason my car was not out front.

Curtis, Terry and the woman left as quickly as they could before the police arrived. He didn't come back for a few days. When I think about it, finding someone in your home violating, is quite an experience and even though my love for him was gone, it was a "pissed me off" experience.

Another time, I had a gut feeling that something was not right. Nothing could have prepared me for what I was about to encounter.

Cashana drove me Poochie, and Diane to the house. She waited outside while the three of us went in. Both Diane and Poochie smoked but knew I didn't like smoke in my house so they put the cigarettes out.

I opened the door and the smell of gas smacked us in the face. Someone left the stove on. As we ventured further in the house I saw feet turned upside down. It was Curtis – passed out lying halfway on the bed and halfway on the floor with a lighter in his hand. The smell of the gas must have knocked him out. I called the police and the three of us ran back outside to the car to wait.

They called an ambulance because he was totally unconscious. The suicide note that he left for whoever would have found us had he been able to ignite the lighter once I walked in the house was lying next to the bed. He was taken to the hospital and I didn't hear any more about him until several days later. I realize now that I should have pressed charges but I was still dealing with the fact that he had full blown AIDS and was probably going to die any day. No need in making his life more miserable than he already was. I was too blinded by pity to see that he was extremely dangerous. He knew he could not come back to the house. He went to Poochie's and Sam's place to stay.

The drug boys got a hold of him one day and beat him to a pulp. He was rushed and admitted to the hospital. His head was swollen, both eyes were black and his jaw was cracked. He was bruised everywhere almost and looked like a monster. He checked himself out after one day's stay.

He went back to Poochie's house but couldn't stay. There was too much confusion with him and Sam. Poochie dropped him at my house. I was angry at her for doing that, but once I saw how damaged he was, I felt really sorry for him. He could stay until he got himself together which was the worst mistake I could've made. Once he got in, he would never leave.

I believed in all we were going through he was dealing with his condition in his own way. I felt sorry for him because I didn't know how long he had to live. He was still smoking crack-cocaine, drinking alcohol and living like he wanted to die. His friends were calculating how long they thought he would live. One or two people thought he would not make it through the year.

A NEW LOOK

Rona and I talked about all that was going on and I guess she was tired for me. Gifted in home decorating, she decided to give the house a makeover. She's also gifted in personal appearance looking 10 years younger. Her eyes dance with kindness and she smiles almost all of the time. Medium height and legs to die for, she worked out off and on for years and looks fabulous for her age. Her voice speaks kindness.

Rona's house, in my opinion, is impeccably beautiful from one end to the other. Whenever I'm there, I'm always looking around.

Sick with the flu the first day she came to work at my house I didn't see how hard and diligent she performed. She and her daughter Brittney and Brittney's cousin BJ were up a couple of mornings until 4:00 a.m. determined to make the living room beautiful.

When done, she took my hand, told me to close my eyes and led me in the living room. I opened them and couldn't talk. The room looked like it should have been in a magazine! She gave the living room a dazzling touch of color with prints and flowers and all kinds of new pictures and arrangements making me look at each section of that room in awe. I couldn't imagine how she came up with the color scheme or any of it!

The room was done in my favorite colors at the time, hunter green, egg plant purple, lavender and beige. She wall papered with flowers and stripes making me think she had bumped her head. But I was wrong! The flowers and stripes came together in that particular color scheme to match perfectly.

The green couch and lavender chairs were in harmony. The throw rug she placed on the floor and the pillows on the couch softly matched the masculine pillows laying on the chairs. The lamps added just enough light in the evening. The window treatments were the same colors as the furniture. She not only knew my personality, she added dashes of what she knew Curtis would like too. Rona was brilliant.

I couldn't figure out how she would decorate the dining room so the only thing I could do was wait to see the results. The window treatments showed tiny touches of red berries and the flower arrangements were handpicked and arranged by her. Understand that when Rona does a flower arrangement, it should definitely be on display. The colors matched perfectly.

The wall paper and pictures gave the dining room a new attitude. The same colors flowed from one room to the other. She fancied the table with candles and one big pretty green and lavender flower arrangement. I didn't know which room I liked the best. I sat and looked around for hours.

Her next project was the bedroom. Rona's husband, at the time Kenny Cook, told her to not do that to herself.

"I know Bunny is your best friend but you have to tell her. There is nothing you can do with that bedroom. She needs professional contractors. It's old with creepy walls. You need to be honest and upfront and leave that room alone."

I have to admit that because the house was old and Curtis' uncle put an unfinished addition on the bedroom, decorating it was going to be tough.

She wallpapered the bedroom and sitting area in an ivory satin stripe that appeared to be silky. The top of the wall paper was a border colored in the same hunter green and eggplant purple as the living room. She shopped and purchased Queen Ann cherry wood chairs that gave a touch of elegance to the room. The foot stool added a whole new flavor. She designed and arranged all of the flowers and hung gorgeous window treatments hiding many of the flaws caused by Curtis' constant beating on the walls. Other areas were decorated with trinkets and pieces of art curbing the eye in several directions at once, making it difficult to decide where to focus. She loved it herself, saying she wish God had given her the same idea for her own bedroom. I hugged her and cried. To me, it was the most beautiful room in the world. I couldn't leave out of that room for the rest of the day.

Rona brought Kenny by to see the bedroom. He sat down, admired the walls, the carpet, the furniture, the colors, the treatments, the tables, the entertainment area and the sitting area and winked his eye.

"Ah, man. This is beautiful. You did a great job!"

As if that was not enough, Michelle's room needed cheering up too. She turned that room into a little girl's dream, lacing it with yellows and greens. Ribbons were strategically placed in unique areas of the room. The window treatments were so beautiful I didn't want anyone to touch them. They connected with the biggest prettiest yellow ribbons you can imagine.

The bedspread must have been handmade for it sat there in its finest yellow, cushioned with what looked like huge pillows. The floor treatments were enough that I didn't want anyone sitting on the bed or wearing shoes. The dolls and pictures matched as did the walls and floors. It was the most beautiful little girl's room I had ever seen. Michelle was in awe and loved it!

Finally, she turned Jasmin's room, which was larger than mine and Michelle's, into a college student's fantasy. The bedside table was decorated with the fanciest of blues and lavenders, to match the halfway wallpaper on the walls. The other part of the wall was painted in crafty sponged colors to match the other pastel colors.

She dressed the bed in blues and lavender to match the walls and hung the most fabulous paintings. How she was able to add a touch of Africa to blues and lavenders, I don't know, but she did. There were throw rugs throughout the room matching the bed and window treatments. Jasmin invited every friend she could think of to our house.

Curtis watched it all and as soon as she left talked about it.

"I can decorate too you know. She ain't done nothing special."

I detected a hint of jealousy and didn't want to cause any friction between the two of them. I wanted to keep peace.

"Oh shoot, I already know you can decorate."

He came in one night angry and fussed about the money spent to decorate. When he asked for money and I said I had none he started slamming the hatchet into the master bedroom wall. With each hit he complained that I should have never spent money to decorate.

I didn't say a word and hoped and prayed that Rona didn't come by to see the mess he made after she worked so hard to make it beautiful. By this time, I was depressed and sick. Besides, I was focusing on Michelle going to see her favorite performer, L'il Bow Wow. The show was sold out.

To my surprise, one of my co-workers, Cynthia Gause, asked if I knew anyone who wanted to go because she had 3 tickets she couldn't use. That would be me! Michelle was going to be the happiest little girl in the world. She was going after all. Thank God for Cynthia Gause!

The day before the show, Jasmin, who agreed to take Michelle and a friend to the event, called to ask what happened to the radio in the car I bought for her to go back and forth to college in. The summer before, she used her money to buy a new state of the art radio for it. The engine was going bad and it was just sitting there.

"Curtis probably took it. I'll call and ask if he did."

In one of the nastiest, meanest voices I ever heard from him he admitted to taking it.

"Yeah, I took it. Why?"

In the background, I could hear things breaking like he was hitting something with the hammer or hatchet.

I got home, saw the damage and did everything I could to maintain my composure. I didn't say much because I had no energy to argue with him. Talking would lead to arguing and arguing would lead to screaming so I just didn't say a thing.

Jasmin, Michelle and I left out of the house and walked a few blocks up the street to Kennisha's, Michelle's cousin. Kennisha, Curtis' step niece was one of those people that can do everything from fixing hair, manicures, waxing eyebrows and making clothes. If she saw you do something once, more than likely she could repeat it.

She was full of personality and had the looks to go with it. Her mother, Fefe was half German and drop dead gorgeous. Kennisha was a close replica. Although many people were confused as to whether or not Kennisha was White or Black, her eyes hypnotized you. Half the time you didn't know if her eyes were green, gray or blue, especially since she didn't wear contacts. Her hair was not quite blonde nor was it brown. She was about 5'4" and had legs to die for. Kennisha was a giving, kind person as long as you didn't mess with her children. The ghetto could and would come out immediately. She was always trying to help the next one. The same with her sister Sabrina who was also drop dead gorgeous. Sabrina is such a beauty that whenever she goes out, she is surrounded by men who just want to have a conversation with her. You ever see the kind of women that just spell sexy? That's Sabrina. I loved those two girls like my own children.

Kennishia fixed Michelle's hair for the L'il Bow Wow show and drove us home. Curtis was in the bedroom in the middle of the mess he created earlier, laying there mumbling and talking with himself and sounding really weird like something out of a horror movie.

I called Poochie on the phone and described what he did to our bedroom. I told her all of the work Rona did in our house he was trying to destroy. Curtis jumped up out of the bed and jumped right in my face like a mad man.

"Don't talk about me or say my name!"

He was leaning back as if to strike me.

"I know you'd better not hit me."

I walked out of the main bedroom into Michelle's bedroom. I continued talking about how tired I was of him and couldn't take it anymore because I felt like a nervous breakdown was coming on. It must have made him mad when he heard me say I've been begging him to get mental help. He followed me and again told me not to mention his name all the while leaning back as if to strike me.

By this time, I was so sick of him I could have thrown up. Before I knew it, he pushed me on the bed, got on top of me and started punching me, beating me in my face. It happened so fast I couldn't believe it or react which is when Jasmin heard the commotion and rushed in the room to help me. She jumped on the bed almost on his back and tried to help but I guess because of how we were positioned the only thing she could do was reach around him and put her hand on my face to prevent what could have been a devastating blow to my teeth. He started punching on Jasmin in her face too.

While I was trying to get up, he managed to snatch my purse and ran out of the room. Michelle was standing there watching the whole thing, screaming to the top of her lungs. I was on my way to get a knife. I was saying out loud "I'ma kill you!" forgetting that Michelle heard everything I was saying. She grabbed me screaming NO! NO! PLEASE DON'T HURT HIM!"

I looked down in her face and realized the drama she was going through. She was crying.

"LOOK AT YOU MOMMY! YOU'RE HURT! YOU'RE HURT!"

I tried to comfort her by saying I was okay. She kept screaming

"NO YOU'RE NOT! LOOK AT YOUR FACE MOMMY! LOOK AT YOUR FACE!"

I must have looked like a monster to her at the time with my swollen eyes and jaws. What I didn't realize was Curtis took my purse that had the L'il Bow Wow tickets and I was positive that he would not bring them back. He would sell the tickets and Michelle would never see Bow Wow.

After comforting Michelle, I saw the phone lying on the floor where I dropped it and was surprised that Poochie was still on the phone. She heard the commotion and was relieved that everything was okay. She called the police. I was still shaking from the altercation and my face felt like it was on fire. I went to the mirror to see how much damage was done and Lord have mercy. How was I going to go to work the next day? The events of the night had just caught up with me. I started crying.

The police took an incident report and suggested I go downtown the next morning to file for a TPO (Temporary Protection Order) and to be careful. I was still shaken and asked if they could wait for us to get in our car to leave the house. We didn't know where Curtis was and for all we knew he could have been hiding out somewhere in the back alley waiting for the police to leave to start everything back over. We left the house, Michelle going to Kennisha's and me and Jasmin going to Poochie's. We didn't want Michelle to be with us if Curtis came to Poochie's starting trouble.

The only thing I could think of all through the night was I was going downtown in the morning to take out a TPO and was issued one immediately.

To my surprise, a woman came to talk to me about battered women. She asked where I was staying and what my plans were.

"I'm staying with my sister but I already know I can't stay there long. There is no way I can go back to my own house. If my husband can't stay there, he would never let me stay there either.

"There are places for women like you and your children."

Of course I doubted it because most people in my salary range were ineligible for any type of programs. She shook her head no. They help anybody. They knew that some women were helpless, even the ones from wealthy environments. Some of those women had no money because it was their husbands' money. I was instructed to come back the next day to the Crime Victims office. I had hope.

When I got to Poochie's that evening Sam almost gave me a nervous breakdown.

"Be careful Bunny. I saw Curtis earlier and he's looking for you and Jasmin with a sawed off shotgun. He said if he gon' die you should die with him. He had nothing to live for and don't want you living either."

The horror inside me was overwhelming. Why did he have to hate so much? Why did he feel I should die too? I never understood why people that wanted to die couldn't do themselves and leave everybody else alone.

I had to tell the people on my job what was going on in case Curtis came looking for me. I believed that no one would be able to stop him if he had a shotgun. They thanked me for the heads up and asked what they could do to help. They would move me across country at their expense if need be. In other words what could they do? These people were in my corner. I told them for the moment, I was too confused to make any decisions but would let them know once I had a chance to think about it.

I went to the Crime Victims section and told them that I basically had nowhere to go.

"We can move you to a hotel for the time being and everything will be paid for. The only thing you need is to just go. Unfortunately, we don't provide transportation nor any food."

I thanked them for their help, hugged the women involved and left. I got to Poochie's, told her that I was unable to let anyone know where I was staying because I didn't want Curtis to somehow or another find out where we were. She understood. Jasmin, Michelle and I left for our new place. Michelle never got to go to the L'il Bow Wow show.

While in the hotel room, my girls and I sneaked in and out of cabs to go to the store or do whatever we had to do. I didn't have a car and needed one bad. The minivan that I use to have was in need of a new transmission. I decided to go to the weekly police car auction.

I noticed a gray Chevrolet that was torn up in the front, obviously in a car wreck. A little voice that only I could hear said to me, "Get that car." The car looked so bad but the voice in my head was insistent. "Bid on that car, bid now." The first bid on the car was $25. I raised my hand.

"How about $50?" Another hand rose. "Can we get $75?" I raised my hand. "How about $100?" Another hand raised. "How about $125?" I raised my hand. "Can we get $150? Can we get $150?" No one raised their hand. "$125 going once. $125 going twice. SOLD!

I took care of the paperwork. To my surprise, the car drove like a baby. There was nothing wrong except it needed cosmetics. A blessing.

After spending a few weeks in the hotel room, the women's group told us we needed to find a place to live because we couldn't stay in the hotel too much longer. We had approximately 2 weeks to find a place. I found an apartment in Maryland and hoped that if I got it Curtis would never suspect me moving to Maryland. He knew I would probably live in DC near my family members.

A hearing for my Civil Protection Order was set. Kathleen Behan, who we called Kitty, one of the partners at my law firm heard about my situation called. She wanted to know who was helping with the Protection Order? She wanted to help."

I thought wow, another blessing with some of the greatest lawyers in the world. God is good.

I initially thought going to court would be a breeze. Curtis knew what he did and should've acknowledged it and moved on. Instead, he too, secured a lawyer, court appointed. He denied everything. He also challenged the claim I had with the insurance company for the damage he did in the house. One of the finest associates in the firm, Mike, was helping Kitty with my case and told me to prepare for trial and keep in mind it would not be easy. I thought to myself, this is going to be awful. I didn't want to look Curtis the monster in the face. I had faced him in enough trials and tribulations already.

The first thing my lawyers asked in our private meeting was, what skeletons were in my closet that I absolutely didn't want anyone to know that Curtis could expose? I knew that my employer and coworkers didn't have a clue that I use to do drugs and never wanted them to know, especially since I had developed the relationship I had with them. I laid that out on the table first and everybody laughed, not that it was funny, it was just that most people at one time or another went through their early days doing something they had no business, whether it was drugs, cigarette smoking, promiscuous sex, driving their parents car, soliciting anything from money to club hopping, the list goes on. They told me that it was not such a good thing, but right now I was clean and had been clean for 11 years. What was next?

I told them I went to Atlantic City regularly on the weekends to get away from the madness and also because I liked to gamble, or so I thought. I explained how I knew just about everybody in the city and it was almost like going to a party in Atlantic City. I knew all of the hustlers, the dealers, the pitt bosses and many regular clients of the casinos. Quite frankly, I enjoyed my ventures on the weekends. Did I lose? Yes. Most of the time but for me it was not all about the gamble. It was being in an environment away from the "bitch" this and "bitch" that. They were writing the whole while I was talking. Next?

That was basically the dirt on me. I knew he was telling people that I slept around in Atlantic City and he thought I gave him AIDS. I had been tested since 1998 and this was 2001. The virus was still not in my system, so there was no possible way I could have given it to him.

The lawyers battled back and forth up until the day of trial. There was so much paper work I thought about what I would have done had Kitty not taken the case.

I was rejected more than once by people who I asked to be witnesses. No one wanted to have the wrath of Curtis on their heads because they knew that he didn't care about living.

Jasmin had to be a witness. She was nervous and couldn't believe that all of this was happening. She hung in there and was ready for battle. Curtis bought in a couple of character witnesses.

Then there was me. I had to give an account of what I had been through living with the monster part of Curtis. My testimony went on for 2 days all for a civil protection order that should have, in my opinion, been issued the minute it was applied for.

Curtis never took the stand. The judge issued the Civil Protection Order with no questions asked. Curtis was so angry that we later learned that the attorney, who represented him in the CPO case, bowed out when it was time for the criminal case.

For a few months after the CPO was issued, I watched every move I made. I watched cars while standing at the corner to make sure no one was rushing to run over me. I looked at people who got too close for fear of having something thrown on me. I denied that I was Sylvia or Bunny if someone thought they recognized me if I didn't know who they were. In others words, I was scared and paranoid. His mother use to tell stories how back in her day she would hide behind trees with a gun, waiting for her boyfriend and shoot at him once he appeared. I thought about how some of his family told me little things they did to their lovers or friends to scare and hurt them. They didn't care and was not afraid of prison. Curtis was no.1 on the list. He would tell you quick he could do the time, anytime. I couldn't continue to live in fear. If he was going to come, bring it on.

Curtis left the area because he heard Steve, my nephew and his boys were looking for him, not because of me, but because of Jasmin. Fighting Jasmin didn't sit well with the family. I didn't have to worry about him so much anymore and was glad to move on with my life, Curtis or no Curtis.

During the holiday season 2001 entertaining was almost the only thing I could think about. I offered to put together a holiday show for our firm. We came up with the Motown Review which would include staff and the partnership. This news drew the biggest crowd of employees in the history of the Firm, so I was told. I had 5 partners, including the managing partner, dressed up like the Temptations singing "My Girl." We changed the words to "My Firm. It was a success and I realized how much I missed being on stage.

2003 – THE CALL

On the way home from work, I had a message on my cell phone. After almost 2 years, I heard Curtis' voice saying he wanted to speak with his daughter and to please give him a call on his cell. He left the number and Michelle almost fainted with excitement.

Suppose this was a trick? What did he want? Was he trying to use Michelle to get back at me? After careful consideration, I thought Michelle at least deserved to find out what he was talking about.

He told us about his new life. He was off drugs and alcohol, spoke to large audiences almost daily about the pitfalls of using drugs and why he quit. He gained a lot of weight. He spoke about his new girlfriend and her daughter. He felt he was doing pretty well. Therapy was one of the best things that happened to him.

The next time we spoke, he put his therapist on the phone. She sounded awfully kind and spoke of the progress she saw in Curtis. She said he spoke often and highly of his family and how he was hoping to reunite with them. She was proud of his disassociation with drugs and alcohol and looked forward to their meetings.

He was proud that she spoke well of him. I could always tell when he was around professional people because he talked "proper."

He came to DC for about 2 weeks with his new girlfriend. Michelle cried when he left but got over it because of the celebration for her birthday. She and I talked about her trip to Michigan and laughed about how jealous Curtis' new girlfriend Misty was.

I called him the next day to make sure he got back okay. When I spoke to him, he had that whisper, get high voice. I knew he had been smoking crack/cocaine and he knew I knew it too. He broke down and told me he had a relapse.

A few months later, he decided it was time to move back to DC. The people in Michigan couldn't wait for Curtis to leave and celebrated his departure. They had one big THANK GOD CURTIS IS GONE celebration. Misty called and told me that she had to be the happiest person in the world. She said she felt sorry for me because all he talked about was making me pay.

"Watch your back, Bunny. Watch your back."

I was trying to think of how I could file for a divorce amicably without any drama. To my surprise, he mentioned it first. He wanted to file but before doing so, wanted to go over the details of our split. What split? We weren't together and hadn't been for years.

"Okay, here's the deal, I want alimony for 24 months. Give me $5,000 in cash up front to help me get myself together. The law is on my side and if you don't agree to my terms, I'm taking you to court and make you pay far more."

I knew then he needed a therapist. I told him to go ahead and take me to court, which is exactly what he did.

Curtis filed papers asking for an absolute divorce and temporary alimony until the actual trial at which time he would ask for life alimony.

Kitty said that the firm didn't do divorces but she would ask around to see if anyone was interested. One associate volunteered and would prove to be one of the finest, smartest, strongest young women in a court of law. I couldn't have asked for a better blessing.

We were scheduled to go to court on November 30, 2004 for the temporary alimony hearing. Suppose they made me pay him every month? Suppose he won? Suppose the law really was on his side?

The associate that worked with me wanted to know everything. She badgered, drilled, and researched whatever she could. I was in awe of her work. She was only 26 years old - the same age as Jasmin. Kitty, the partner overseeing the case, was in a horrible car accident. She was air lifted to a hospital. Not only was she overseeing my case, she was my friend. I prayed for her recovery and kept her in my prayers.

SUPERIOR COURT OF THE DISTRICT OF COLUMBIA

There's a certain smell in a courtroom. Almost like the smell of wood furniture. No matter what I'm going to court for, anxiety is present.

I was sick with nervousness. The judge reviewed Curtis' complaint and told us to wait for her decision about the alimony payments and the scheduling order for a trial.

"I see that this case is not going to be amicably resolved. The pre-trial notice is set for January 30, 2005. No temporary alimony allowed."

That was good for me. I'm not sure if I would have been able to send that man a check every month until this was over so I was happy to hear that verdict. It was a long wait through the holidays.

Word was going around town that he was borrowing large sums of money from people insuring them that once he got a settlement from the divorce he would pay them back. The word was the least he would get would be $50,000. He was looking for far more than that and estimated that after he got half my 401k, half of the insurance proceeds I was paid as a result of the house being destroyed, half the value of the current house I was in and half the value of the house at 1016 Douglas Street, NE, he was looking at around $500,000. He had all of his family and friends excited.

The trial was set for June 13th and 14th with me having 4 hours to present my case and Curtis with 8. He originally asked for 3 days as if we were Mr. & Mrs. Donald Trump.

Curtis presented me with document production requests, answers he was looking for about money and anything he could think of. Although I basically asked for the same, my number one request was to find out when and how he became infected with HIV/AIDS.

I submitted everything involving my financial life. My lawyers wanted everything squeaky clean. Curtis on the other hand didn't answer his interrogatories properly. He failed to produce documents and generally didn't participate. We had to drag and pull answers out of him.

I gave him all kinds of evidence including tax forms, bank records, telephone records, cell phone records, earnings and anything that had to do with money. He wanted to see exactly how much money I made and what I was doing with it. He wanted all evidence including any gambling and hotel records. He also asked for employee attendance records, all assets and places of employment. He asked for items he didn't need just in case.

On the day of the trial, I thought about the old days when I was performing. I missed that part of my life. I met with the attorneys who walked with me to the courthouse. We were all a little nervous but up for the fight. I felt sick again. There was Curtis pulling a box with folders and more folders of documents.

The judge continued with the divorce proceeding. Curtis had to prove his case. As we proceeded, he took the longest time not only asking his questions, but looking for documents to make his points.

"Sylvia, tell the court how I was abusive?"

"One night you came in the bedroom and demanded money. I didn't have any. You insisted I had money somewhere."

I looked at the judge to explain the story to her as he watched. He was not sure where I was going with my testimony.

"That night he argued for so long about money he looked at my fingers and told me to give him my wedding rings. To avoid any further argument and any possible physical confrontation, coupled with the fact that I was exhausted, I gave him the rings. He sold them for $10."

He asked more questions that were damaging to his case. The judge looked at us like "are you serious?" She stopped the proceedings.

"Do you really want to continue with this line of questioning sir?"

It was almost as if she was trying to help him, acting as his lawyer. Was she on his side?

We were out of time. The judge gave us a new date to finish. I almost cried when she said August 30. I would have to wait through the entire summer. I went home that night and thanked God that at least my testimony was over. Because of the extended date, Curtis had a whole 2 months to figure out what he would say in his closing argument. I just wanted this over, quickly and as soon as possible.

BACK TO BACK IN THE DAY

Leaving out of the bank, I heard a voice.

"Oh, you're not gonna speak?"

Steve Haynes was standing there in the flesh. An old friend from my Cocoran Street days, I always thought Steve was handsome. His eyes were dark and so was his mustache and hair. He was about 5'7" and muscular, obviously not as muscular was he was back in the day. He still looked good. You could tell he worked out. One of my fondest and funniest memories was when we were kids. Poochie kissed Steve while hiding with him in a dingy garage up the street from our house playing hide and seek. A strange bug was crawling on her. She thought it was a sperm. She told Ma she was pregnant and Ma had to laugh at that one herself. I wanted to tell Steve why I was smiling but opted not to considering he was with a woman, who happened to be his wife.

We talked about Stead Playground at 17th & P Streets, where all of the kids hung out back in the day with the exception of me and Poochie. We could only go if escorted by an adult. We talked about Ma, Peter's pool table where all the guys in the neighborhood gathered to play. We talked about how David Reavis died over a $5 rock of crack. How some of the other guys who were either killed, died from drugs or were still hanging around doing nothing. We both couldn't believe how 2 of the most popular guys in the neighborhood, Larry Ring and Stanley Johnson died and how horrific some of the deaths were or the conditions some of them were living in. Most of the guys from our neighborhood at one time or another played some type of sport. I immediately thought of my experience with Larry and the NBA. I know nothing about sports anymore. When I met Gilbert Arenas of the Washington Wizards I had no clue who he was. Stevie, my nephew had to tell me it was him when he stopped at our table to say hello. I still didn't know and didn't care.

Steve said people had been following my career and wondered what happened to me. Some thought I died and many knew of my association with drugs and brushed me off saying what a shame it was I let myself go.

We bid our farewells and exchanged numbers promising to keep in touch.

Shortly after that I ran into Kenny Jones, Radar's cousin.

I was heading to get some lunch to take back to the office and there he was walking toward me. We both smiled greeting each other with a hug. We laughed talking about the old days for the longest time. He told me that Radar's son, Rico, had been killed. Apparently someone stabbed him several times, in an unnecessary altercation. I again thought of David Reavis.

I was reminded he married Pat Williams, one of the girls that made the cheerleading squad the year I was cut. He told me how he and Pat broke up, which bought to mind my upcoming divorce. Pat was involved in the drug world, started spending all of his money and stealing.

"I came home and caught a man in the house. I wanted to kill him, but my gut told me to walk away. I did."

I had flashbacks about my own incident.

A year later, Pat was found dead in one of the prostitution houses on Rhode Island Avenue in NE Washington overdosed from a shot of heroin. I could see the sadness in his eyes when he spoke about it but he soon came back to life. Although he and Pat divorced before she died, unlike me, no alimony or suits were involved. They had no kids and the divorce went through with no drama. He was glad to be done with that whole era of his life and happy about his new wife Bea.

We talked about Radar a little more and I was happy to hear how well he was doing.

"Send me the information regarding Rico."

Kenny emailed the information. I wanted to go and offer my condolences. I wanted to be there for him. I knew he would be surprised, if he remembered me. It had been over 30 years since I last saw him.

I left work and went straight to the funeral home. I sat outside in my car, windows up and the air conditioning running, and watched people go in and out of the funeral home hoping I would recognize Radar before I went in. It felt a little strange being there after not having seen Veronica, Rico's mother, since high school. I gathered my things, turned off the car, checked the mirror one more time to make sure the little make up I had on was in tact and proceeded to the funeral home. I had not seen Del Rico since he was a baby and had no recollection of him at all.

I walked in the funeral home with still no signs of Radar and headed to the casket. I took a long look at Del Rico. My heart was aching for him and his mother and father.

I turned to leave the casket and there she was. Veronica was standing there looking at me smiling. Her tears were evident. We hugged. I could see she was hurting from all she was going through.

"Bunny, it's been so long! How are you?"

I almost couldn't answer her I was so choked. Her tears were getting bigger but she was smiling. I had to hurry and answer. I didn't want to bust out crying. She was obviously devastated.

"I am so sorry to hear of your loss Veronica. I can't imagine what you may be going through right now and quite honestly, I don't know what to say. When I heard about what happened, I had to come, I just had to."

She politely thanked me and we hugged again. After another quick chat she asked had I seen Radar. Veronica remembered how close Radar and I were at one time and I appreciated her asking. I was embarrassed that I wasn't sure if I had seen him or not because like I said, people change over the years. Suppose he had gained a lot of weight or was gray? Had I seen him and didn't know it was him?

"He just left to go outside"

I walked to the front door of the funeral home and looked around. I didn't see anyone I knew so I decided to go outside to get some air. Before I had a chance to breathe good, I lost my breath. There he was! Aside from a little weight gain and a tiny bit of gray on the sides, Radar had not changed. He looked at me like he didn't know who I was, but I was wrong. He knew exactly who I was.

"Sylvia Morrison - oh my goodness!" I smiled.

He grabbed me and we hugged for a long time. I offered my condolences and just looked at him for a moment. A warm feeling came over me. He crept into my thoughts often. He was my history - and my first boyfriend. He must have known what I was thinking.

"I was thinking about you just recently and all the fun we use to have at Ms. Betty's. Man, nobody gave parties like y'all. How's Pete?

I was sorry to hear he lost his mother. I use to love Ms. Jones. No matter what was going on, she was always nice to me.

"How did you know to come here?"

"I saw your cousin Kenny Jones and he told me what happened."

He paused a moment, like he was in deep thought.

"I was crazy about you back then but I had to play the role especially when you broke up with me. I thought I was gonna loose my mind."

"Are you serious?"

"Man, hell yeah. It killed me because if I showed how crazy I was about you the fellas would have made fun of me and you know I wasn't havin' that. I was too much of a playa back then."

We both laughed. I thought back to that very day when I was sick with heartache and wondered how things would have turned out had he made up with me and took me off into the sunset. My thoughts were interrupted because many people stopped to offer condolences, give hugs, cards, smiles, and jokes, whatever.

Kenny and his wife joined us in conversation. It was a pleasure meeting Bea. I felt close to her for some reason. Radar's wife, daughter and grandson walked in.

Lynn Jones was a fly and attractive woman. Her well attended to hair and brown roasted complexion made the 2 piece white suit she was wearing stand out. She flashed a sassy smile which also shared her confidence. Her eyes were bright, yet concerned. The little make up she wore was almost invisible. Unsurprisingly, she was very friendly. Her eyes started sparkling. He introduced us and we hugged. Radar motioned he was going inside.

After talking with Kenny and Bea for a while, I felt I should leave, especially since Veronica was out in the lobby area crying. My heart couldn't take it. I wished there was something I could do for her but knew that I had nothing to offer but my condolences.

I said a silent prayer and walked back to the sanctuary to bid my farewells. We all exchanged numbers and email addresses and I promised we would get together soon. On the way out, I saw Lynn who grabbed my hand, flashed that sassy smile and stood up to say farewell. I thought to myself, what a lady.

THE FINAL DIVORCE

I was ready to hear the verdict. I thought of all that I went through with Curtis. I questioned how I was able to stay in such madness. We had been married exactly 10 years.

I thought of my bout with ulcerative colitis. When my colon acted up, I threw up, had headaches and felt so bad that I wondered if I would be better off dead. I was told my entire colon was infected and had to be removed. I would have to live with a bag on the outside of my body for the rest of my life. I was 27 years old at the time.

During that time, patients discussed with me life in that capacity. Although I admired their courage and strength I was just not mentally prepared to go through the trauma, especially since I was still dealing with the death of my parents and the whole Larry thing.

That night, I went into the tiny bathroom in my hospital room, got on my knees and prayed that God would find a way to eliminate the major surgery taking place that next morning. If the surgery was a must then so be it, but I was not about to give up on a spiritual fight.

At 7:00 am the surgeon requested a new x-ray. He placed the x-ray from the day before on the board for review. The magnitude of the surgery was huge and he wanted to be sure. Once the new x-ray returned he placed it alongside the one from the day before.

The new x-ray revealed only 6 inches of damaged colon. They were clearly different pictures. The technician, who took both x-rays, assured the surgeon that I was the only person that took that type of x-ray the day before and that morning, so it had to be me.

The second x-ray was correct. They removed 6 inches. I wear the scar from the surgery, but not the bag.

How about the thyroid diagnosis? The goiter on the front of my neck was so big it looked like a mini golf ball. Any infection would send me straight to the hospital and I would be in there for several days at a time.

The options were I could have the surgery to remove the goiter or take a once in a lifetime dosage of radioactive iodine. I chose the iodine. I couldn't take a chance on surgery for fear of losing my ability to do impressions or sing again. I signed papers that said I would never be able to have any more children. They administered the iodine. And again, I was not supposed to ever be able to have children. 12 years later I delivered Michelle. Although the iodine took its effect, the obstetrician I was seeing sold me on a drug, unauthorized by the Food and Drug Administration that would build a bed in my womb to save the baby. Michelle is one hot chick today!

I thought about how I found Regina dead and could have walked in on the murder.

I reminisced on the blessed delivery from drugs and cigarettes.

I thought about the AIDS incident and how I could really never be angry about anything considering I was unaffected by that disease.

There was the day I ran out of the office to go to the bank which was only a block and a half away. I didn't have much time because I had to get back to the office since it wasn't my lunch hour. People on the street who ask for money use to bother me because I always thought that if they had time to beg, they could get a job. My thinking would change based on that day's series of events. A woman, standing on the sidewalk asking for money, singled me out.

"Miss, Miss – excuse me Miss?"

I tried to ignore her but she was insistent. "Miss, Miss?" I answered – "Yes?"

"Can you give me a quarter please?"

For whatever reason, something told me to stop to give her the quarter. She told me she had seen me many times. She rode the bus with me once too. We talked for about 5 minutes. I enjoyed my short conversation with her and realized I was supposed to be going to the bank so I bid her a good day and rushed up the street to the bank. To my surprise, police were everywhere. Someone had just robbed the bank. Had I not stopped to give the woman the quarter, I would have been in the middle of the robbery. I know this is weird but this is what happened next.

We were told to go to the next closest bank on New York Avenue which was about 6 or 7 blocks away. It was imperative that I go because I had a deposit I had to make. On the way I saw a man who called me out just like the woman.

"Miss, Miss? Excuse me, Miss? You got a quarter?"

I had this eerie feeling and figured I had nothing to lose by giving him a quarter, considering the quarter I just gave the woman saved me from a bank robbery. I gave him the quarter and proceeded to tell him about the incident that just happened. We talked a little longer than I planned so I bid him a good day.

By the time I got to the bank on New York Avenue, you ready? That bank had just been robbed as well. I couldn't believe it. I just stopped for a minute to collect my thoughts. Fifty cents saved me from 2 bank robberies.

My attitude has changed toward people when they ask for money. What's really strange is that sometimes when I walk by, many times that person holds their head down and doesn't even ask me. I don't know what that's all about but now, whenever anyone calls me out for change, I stop and give it to them.

All of these thoughts were running through my head when the judge welcomed us back to her court room. She told Curtis to finish his closing argument with only information she had not heard before. Every time he said something, the judge would say something like "and we've heard that too." We could detect the frustration in his closing and he finally decided that he had nothing else to say.

The judge did not leave the room to think about a decision or what she was going to say because she dove right in. My mouth was practically open the whole while she spoke, something to this effect.

"Mr. Pitt, you have presented your case before this court and I've listened carefully. You have stated what you believe you are entitled to and quite frankly I can't believe it. You are no victim here sir. You wreaked havoc in this woman's life. What on earth makes you think you are entitled to something? You get nothing in this divorce, nothing. You deserve nothing. Not one thing!"

I was numb. I looked at my attorneys with wide eyes. They looked at me! I smiled! They smiled! I hugged them and they hugged me back.

I looked the judge straight in her eyes and she looked in mine. I was so overwhelmed I almost couldn't say anything but I looked up in the sky, looked back at her.

"Thank you. Thank you very much your Honor."

She went on about finishing the business of our divorce and granted it that day. Curtis got nothing.

I wanted to scream! Jump with joy and run around the court room thanking God. My lawyers looked at me and smiled again. We were victorious the whole way.

Curtis was obviously disappointed and vowed an appeal out loud. I could hear him mumbling under his breath how the legal system was some bull and he was coming back.

5 years of divorce court and I was finally getting my life back.

On the way home that night I thought about Radar again and all of my high school friends. I thought about the Passions and Soul Poppa, Spelman and my stint with the airlines. I thought about Regina Simms who had been dead for a long time. Tears rolled down my face when I thought about my parents.

I thought about David Reavis' death and my own drug association. I thought about the pageants and the friends I got as a result.

I missed the stage and performing.

THE ACCIDENT

It was quiet and still early in the evening with the breezes coming and going as they pleased. The fireflies were flying about doing what they do. The trees were calm even though the wind was blowing. I had to pick up Michelle, who was 13 from a girlfriend. That meant getting Kamy, my 2 year old granddaughter together.

Kamy, a feisty, adorable smart little girl was the person who made me understand the definition of "apple of my eye." She changed my life when she entered this world. I thought my own kids were special, but this granddaughter was a different breed of special. She was like a little me, two generations down. I looked at her and saw myself. She was a little tall for her age, but a caramel colored doll baby. Her wide eyes focused wherever she set them and her hugs were worth over a million dollars each. This baby loved me unconditionally and I loved it when it was my turn to watch her.

I put her in the new, navy blue state of the art car seat that buckled everywhere. My friend Tamara gave it to me as a gift. This seat assured that if an accident occurred, its occupant was going nowhere.

"Where are we going grandma?"

"We're going to pick up Michelle."

I didn't want Michelle traveling on public transportation alone at 7:00 in the evening. Besides, she was every mother's dream. She did well in school with a 3.86 grade point average. She was extremely respectful to all of my friends and family and everyone she met thought she was a wonderful kid. Her eye lashes were long and dark and her gigantic dark eyes were so big they seemed to take forever to blink. When they did, it was almost as if they struggled to reopen. The sparkle in them made you think of diamonds.

According to my friends, she had an everlasting smile. Most people thought she had tracks in her hair to lengthen and thicken it but that was not the case. Her long legs and skinny arms almost made her look like a stick but her fortunate height along with tiny bits of weight here and there made her an excellent candidate for modeling. She loved rehearsals and trying out for modeling teams preparing early for the great Tyra Banks and America's Next Top Model.

Her McDonald's French fry complexion showed flawless skin. She attracted a lot of guys. They were calling or trying to get a number from her daily. The shout-outs were off the Richter scale and I was thinking to myself "please don't let her fall for any of these guys anytime soon. I don't need any more grandbabies right now." I didn't believe she was doing anything but, well, you know how mothers are and you know how teenagers are.

Michelle is the high maintenance queen. She wants her hair done and hands manicured. Her school uniform, must match. She sends out requests for what she wants, needs and should have. I suggested a job.

After locking Kamy in, I got in the driver's seat of the fairly new metallic silver SUV that offered a comfortable ride. The seats were high enough for me to see over traffic and the comfort of the position of the seat was perfect.

The weather was wonderful this particular evening and the ride was airy. Wind was traveling directly to the back seat where Kamy was sitting so I decided to put the window up to avoid the wind blowing in her face, not knowing that performing that one little single move would save my life.

I came to a stop sign at the entrance of 54th and Nannie Helen Burroughs. People were buzzing on each corner. You saw brothers on the corner doing anything from selling drugs to bootleg movies. Teens traveled in groups going nowhere but to each other's houses. There were guys smoking cigarettes talking about the old times all the while watching females in tight jeans or other fancy clothes. It was an intersection that was extremely busy. There were no street lights. People were dodging between traffic trying to cross the busy intersection and some people took their time getting across the street, secretly hoping to get hit so that they could collect insurance money.

I proceeded into the six lane intersection to make the left turn, not seeing the cars coming from my right. I was forced to stop dead center of the intersection to let the cars go by. I looked to my left and saw oncoming traffic. There was one car traveling at what seemed like lightning speed. Why was he driving so fast? Was he running from the drug boys or was he running to his girl? Was he just somebody who liked to drive fast? Did he see me? I looked back to my right to try to hurry to get out of the speeding car's way but the car to my right was just passing.

Everything went black.

Based completely on bystanders, witnesses, Kamy and court documents, this is what I am told happened that beautiful night in August of 2006. I didn't remember anything until later:

A navy blue Yukon hit my SUV on the driver's side right between the front and back passenger door, missing the driver's door by inches. The vehicle flipped over and landed on the passenger side. The driver of the Yukon appeared to have been drunk because of his swaying and nodding. He kept going.

He was obviously speeding. It didn't matter to him that Kamy and I might be dead. He didn't know us and was not about to find out if we were okay because the scene was obviously one of death. Papers and magazines were strewn about the street. Clothes that were in the trunk area were now stretched across the street and sidewalks. The wheels were still spinning. The SUV looked like it was asleep except for one thing. Smoke was everywhere and gas was leaking out of the tank.

Again, according to court documents and testimonies from witnesses, etc., the Yukon driver thought the SUV might blow up and kill more people. Surely the woman driving that SUV was dead he thought. Dead. He had never been around a dead person except at a funeral and they were eerie. He couldn't bring himself to face a dead person. He had certainly never killed anyone. Driving on a suspended license would automatically get him arrested. He saw people coming from everywhere and said, no, I can not get arrested. I killed somebody. Do I stay? Do I leave? I'm going to jail if I stay. He put his foot to the peddle of the Yukon to speed from out of the area hoping no one got his tag number. He had no clue that a police officer, in plain clothes, saw the accident and chased him.

Another guy who was in court said you could hear women who got out of their cars to see the horrific scene pleading for somebody to help Kamy who was lying in an awkward position on the floor, crying.

He said he wondered who was going to get a baby out of a big truck that might blow up at any moment.

He said a 17 year old Black kid dressed in baggy jeans and tennis shoes saw the whole accident. He was a small kid, not more than 5 feet 7 inches tall but very skinny. He had bright eyes that were shaped like almonds. His hands were in his pockets but his face was sad. The thought of a baby dying was unbearable and he just couldn't let that happen. He wiped the sweat from his forehead. He spit the old chewing gum he had for hours out on the ground. He looked at his watch and thought about the time. He started pacing. He couldn't let Kamy die. That could have been a little kid in the SUV that he knew. He thought about his little sister. He stopped dead in his tracks, looked in the air and decided to go for it. There was no other choice.

His mind quickly calculated how he was going to get her. The best thing he could do was go through the back windshield and crawl in. He looked around for something to smash the back window. There it was, right in his face, a red brick twice the size of his hand. He picked it up and debated if it would work. He tossed it slightly in the air. It was a heavy brick covered with dust and dirt, with little holes from being out in the street. Time and weather had treated the brick with no love but it still held its strength. This was exactly what he needed. He took the brick and rushed to the back of the SUV with quickness. He hoped this was the right way to do this. His eyebrows lifted, one higher than the other. The frown in the middle of both brows became evident.

With a rush of strength from his little frail arm he held the brick up in the air with his right hand positioning it behind his head to the right of his body, the weight of it pulling at his biceps. He had to muster enough strength to throw it just right so that glass would not splatter everywhere, especially on the baby.

His heart was beating so fast that he thought it would pop out of his chest. His eyes started blinking. His legs were stiff. He had to do this just right to keep everything in perspective. With precision, like he was trying to hit a wild lion in the right place on his head, he hit the back window of the SUV with the brick. Glass broke but thank God none got near Kamy to do any damage. The brick made enough of a dent in the window for him to move the rest of the glass with his elbow. He created a hole big enough for him to get through. He didn't care if he got cut. He had to hurry. Enough time had passed already.

He crawled through the hole with some of the glass tearing at his sweat shirt that read "Hip Hop is Not Dead!" The rip that tore at the elbow of the sweat shirt scared him at first because the glass was sparkling with danger. He had no time to be scared. He must move quickly. He hit his knee on another piece of glass that was sticking out and although it hurt it didn't cut him. He proceeded through the hole.

His eyes met Kamy's. His heart seemed to beat faster. She stopped crying. He smiled at her. She smiled back at him. Some super hero was there to save her and she was happy.

In a calming voice that belied his years he said, "Don't worry sweetheart. I'm going to get you out of here, okay?"

Although she didn't answer, her eyes told him that she understood. What was the sparkly stuff all around her? Should she touch it?

"No, don't touch that okay? That's glass and it might cut you."

She obeyed, feeling she was safe. He crawled closer to her in order to get to the seat belt that she was securely strapped in.

"Somebody did a good job of locking you in here little girl. They had you down" he said in a whispery, out of breath voice.

He started breathing harder and sweating profusely. His adrenaline was at the high end because it was dark and he could hardly see how to undo the seatbelt. He fidgeted around the release trying to undo the lock which was almost like trying to undo handcuffs in the blind.

The motor of the truck was still running allowing the sunroof to open with just the touch of a button. "Thank God for some of these new vehicles," he thought to himself. The sunroof was slowly opening and the boy was patient. Kamy was looking at him, trying to figure out who he was but thankful that he took her out of the awkward scary position. She wanted to cry again but opted not to because she couldn't figure out exactly what she wanted to cry for. She was scared but a little happy, unsure of what she was suppose to feel. She stared at him.

He backed out through the hole that he made with the brick but didn't take Kamy with him because he didn't want her to get cut on any of the glass. She saw him leave and started crying thinking he was going to leave her.

"Don't cry okay? I'm just going to get you out another way." He rushed to the outside of the car and reached down through the sunroof. She saw him appear and stopped crying. The sunroof was just big enough to pull her through.

"You gonna get my grandma?"

He didn't respond. He wanted to get her out of the car. They were still in a lot of danger. He grabbed her under both arms and pulled her up through the sunroof, careful not to hit her head or any parts of her body. She was such a small fragile little thing and he wanted her to be safe. He held her in his right hand and arm and pressed her close to him. He put his left hand on her back so that she would not fall backwards. People outside of the SUV practically screamed with delight happy to see Kamy was out of the vehicle and alright. He rushed her away from the truck out of danger's way.

While walking away from the truck he asked Kamy "So that's your grandma in that truck?"

She was too nervous and happy to respond.

"What's your name?"

"Kamy."

What was he going to do with her? There was no one there that knew her or me.

The young man was concerned about me sitting almost upside down in the SUV. Suppose it blew up? It would be a shame if Kamy grew up learning that I could have been saved but wasn't. He didn't care that I was already dead, he just wanted me out, at least that's what he told people.

He ran back to the SUV and climbed up to the driver's front door to open it. He knew that whatever he was going to do he had to do it quickly. He didn't want to blow up either.

He got the door opened and pushed it out as far as it could go. He looked at me. I was completely limp. Fortunately I was strapped in my seat belt otherwise there was no telling where I may have ended up when the car flipped. He looked at my face and noticed that the left side of it was huge.

"She must have hit her head on the window and that must have been what killed her" he told one of the bystanders. He saw the smoke outside of the vehicle getting thicker. He had to hurry.

He reached over me and almost fell into the truck trying to unlatch the seat belt. It unfastened. He grabbed me around my waist and used every ounce of his strength to pull my 170+ pound body out of the seat. The first 2 tries didn't work. I kept falling back into my seat because his strength would not allow him to pull me all the way out. But wait a minute! My hands moved! My arms were reaching around in the air.

"She's alive! Oh my God she's alive!" Knowing I was alive must have given him a boost of energy. He took one good pull and lifted me away from my seat enough to pull me out of the car. He said had he not been able to get me out that time, he was not sure if he would have been able to continue to try. He dragged me to safety on the side of the street. He could hear the sirens of an ambulance in the distance. By now many people had gathered on the streets. People were crying and holding each other because both Kamy and I were out of the vehicle, alive.

The ambulance personnel jumped out and immediately grabbed both me and Kamy.

"Can you hear me m'am? Can you hear me?"

The whole while they were talking they were locking me down on a gurney and started an IV. They braced my neck, back and torso to insure no further damage. They didn't know about the concussion yet. I put the window up to stop the wind from blowing in Kamy's face just in time. Had I left the window down, the jolt from the collision would have snapped my neck and I probably would have died on the spot.

"What's your name m'am?"

"Sylvia."

"Do you know what happened to you?"

"No. Where's Kamy?"

Kamy didn't have a scratch on her body. Not even a smudge. A little shook up maybe, trying to figure out what on earth happened to her and her grandmother but nonetheless just fine. The ambulance driver sat Kamy in the back of the ambulance facing me. They wanted me to physically see for myself that she was fine.

"She's right here m'am, sitting right in front of you."

"Where are the people that were in the accident? Are they dead? I started crying hysterically. I killed somebody?

"We don't know m'am. They hit you and ran. Probably some young kids that stole a car."

I didn't believe them. They were saying that to try to calm me down. I started screaming to the top of my lungs. This was one of my worst nightmares.

"You need to calm yourself down m'am. That's the only way you're going to recuperate from your injuries."

"But they're dead. They're dead. Oh GOD!"

"No they're not. They hit you and ran. They cared nothing about you or the baby."

The tears were coming and I thought about what they said. The side of my face felt like it was being pressed up against some iron and steel.

The 17 year old who saved us was gone. No one got his name or saw where he went. No one knew who he was. It was only because some people talked to him that we know his part of this story.

Jasmin, my oldest daughter, had been notified by the police that an accident had taken place and was told what hospital Kamy and I were being taken too. Jasmin stood 5'10" tall and looked exactly like me. He eyes were dark and spoke kindness yet firmness at the same time. Her smile simply shined and although she didn't smile much, her concern for others spoke volumes. She was physically in almost perfect proportions for her height making her a prime candidate for Calvin Klein jean commercials. Her arms were perfect for any kind of commercial that had anything to do with hands or arms or shoulders. She was born with a kind spirit and most of her friends were close. She sometimes had to turn off her phone because of the many calls that sought her advice and comforting voice. If Jasmin told you something, whether you wanted to hear it or not, you could generally count on it being the truth.

I saw FEAR in her face because she didn't know the extent of the accident or what happened. She later told me that she didn't know if I would pull through the accident but prayed as hard as she could.

The medical assistant in the ambulance unlatched Kamy who ran to Jasmin happy as ever to see her mother. Jasmin looked at me concerned.

"Ma, are you okay? The people who hit you fled the scene. "

Thank God. The people were not dead.

You could see in Jasmin's face that she was thankful to God that two of the most important women in her life, her daughter and her mother, were alive from one of the most horrific accidents the District of Columbia had ever seen.

COMING BACK

The accident was a wakeup call. It showed me that I had another chance, another opportunity. I understand what God did. It took all of these years but now I see it clearly.

I had to go back out and hit the pavements. I needed to see what was happening on the new streets, the today streets. I decided to try my hand at producing and directing by taking on my good friend Shebah's project, "Dear Ancestors, Love Muffin." It was the story of a young 17 year old princess who went to sleep in the 17th Century and woke up today. Shocked at the revelations of what was happening to and with her people, she began to write letters to her ancestors. I was fascinated with her work. I made suggestions as to what I thought would help to bring it to life. She said I gave it too much life because it was a very serious, sensitive matter and needed to be exposed as such. In the interim, a friend, Nyota "Linda" Washington, introduced me to Ty Gray-El, a unique poet, by way of email. I invited him to see Dear Ancestors, Love Muffin.

I introduced him at one of Shebah's shows. I couldn't believe it. He was fascinating! Although he never saw me perform, he insisted I travel with him to Oakland, California as he was asked to appear at the Black Repertory Theatre. He said he had a feeling. We put together a production entitled "The Fifth Commandment Tour" and took it around to several different churches. It was getting rave reviews and many standing ovations. Ty was one of the most incredible, brilliant artists I'd ever met in my life. He is the author of the poem "A Black Woman's Smile" which has been racing the internet with over 3,000,000 collective views on Youtube.

The bug that haunted me for so long was back. I was also checking out the comedy circuit.

I spoke with a couple of my friends from back in the day, Chris Thomas, former BET Mayor of Rap City and Judge Greg Poole, one of my all time favorite comedians and asked if they would be my guests for a show I was putting together entitled "An Evening With Sylvia & Friends." They were down.

I learned from Greg that there were a few open mikes in the area, unlike how it was back in the day. He invited me down to a spot in Georgetown to try my hand at the mike. One of the first people I was reintroduced to was Tony Woods. I couldn't believe I had not seen him in almost 20 years. He went from being a newby to one of the finest.

I ran into Danny Williams who I remembered from the early 70s. He use to wear his hair in a big ol' Jackson 5 afro. I almost didn't know who he was because his hair was cut. He warmed my heart. No sooner than I finished talking with him, in walks Kevin Anthony. Kevin was funny crazy.

I learned about a couple of other open mikes and couldn't believe that the DMV (District, Maryland and Virginia…yeah, yeah, yeah, I had to learn that language too) had all of this action going on in comedy rooms.

Chris called and asked if I could do a feature spot at a club called Club Elite's LOL. By this time, the importance of being a feature as opposed to a headliner had no meaning to me. I had approximately 5 minutes of new relevant material. I had no idea that many people from back in the day would show up for my show.

Andy Evans walked up and I was overwhelmed because when I think about it, Andy was sort of like the only mentor I had. He took his time to explain things in the business and generally had suggestions for me. He was writing and producing and had published a couple of books. They now called him the Counselor of Comedy. I almost had tears in my eyes from happiness. I'm sure Andy questioned why I was working a major urban comedy club with hardly any time.

I started hearing about Facebook but because I was old school I swore I'd never get on it. I thought it was for kids, not knowing that it would soon blow up to one of the biggest internet social networks in the world. My friend Carla kept pushing me to get an account.

"Sylvia, just try it. You're gonna love it."

I got an account and starting requesting most of Jasmin's friends from Eastern High School in DC and found a few family members. I looked for a few people I knew from back in the day like Robin Montague. She was still in comedy and doing well.

Kevin Anthony became my Facebook friend as well as Vincent Cook who was living in California working with Will Smith in some of his movies.

I saw a comment by a guy named Ol' Mike B. I requested his friendship and he accepted! I was so excited. He had a partner by the name of Wayne Manigo so I requested him too. He accepted my friendship as well. They listed where they were performing. Tashya Tummings was hosting a room in Largo, Maryland. I stopped by.

I didn't know anyone there so I asked Tashya if I could get on. She looked at the list and wrote my name down. I felt a little awkward because I knew that half of those kids looked at me and said "who is this old woman?"

She introduced a woman who I thought was pretty big in the comedy world because they said Ayanna Dookie just recently opened for Tommy Davidson and she was doing a lot in the area.

A couple more comics came on and then this one guy, Terence the Comedian got a hold of the microphone and I thought to myself, wow, this guy has it all! He's handsome, charming AND funny.

They called comic after comic, including a guy named Lawrence Owens who stayed on the microphone for about 40 minutes. I was getting impatient because although the audience laughed hard they were thinning out.

When he was done, clearly the star of the night, I remember Chubby told me about the time she met him at his job and told him about me. He asked "Is she funny? Tell her I said to stop by LOL on a Thursday." I mentioned that conversation to him. "I don't remember." He turned away, arrogant like. I said okay and walked away, not knowing that one day he would become one of my favorite comics.

I was last on the list with about 10 people left in the audience. Terence and several of his friends were leaving as I was about to start my set. When he heard the Mo'Nique impression he stopped dead in his tracks, told his buddies to hold up and sat down in the nearest seat. That one little move reminded me of the Ibex back in the day, how people would stop to watch.

Terence and I exchanged numbers. He told me where the comedy room action was. I could not believe there were that many rooms in the DMV compared to how I came up.

I started seeing different people and comics around the clubs and as I worked on my set. I knew that in order for me to grow, I had to do as many rooms as possible. The chatter started around town that Sylvia was back. The vets from back in the day started coming out to see me.

This was scary. I only had 10 minutes worth of material, and based on that I started getting paid jobs. What was I going to do when they wanted a half hour?

My Facebook connections were growing and when I realized I had over 300 friends I was elated! 75% of them were comics and they were posting every show that came their way. I was right there with them too, looking to learn what I could from the youngsters.

Chris was hosting a place called Martini's in Ft. Washington, Maryland and insisted I come out to perform. It was a paid gig and he was sure the people would love me. When I got to the room, it was all Black people, straight from the hood. They wanted to hear rough comedy. Everybody that went on before me gave them exactly what they wanted. They cursed and screamed, stomped, joned and included the audience on almost everything they said. "How many ladies tonight are wearing real bona fide weaves? How many got on they body magic?" (Yes, "they" body magic!) They said and asked anything and the people loved it.

Chris saved me for last. I had no clue why. I prayed the audience would like all 10 minutes of it. It was just like back in the old days. I don't know if people shut up out of respect because I'm older or if they were just being nice. But I felt them with me. By the time I got to the Whoopi Goldberg impression, they were laughing and clapping. They loved Diana Ross. I closed with the Tina Turner impression.

The applause was thunderous and the audience was hollering. There was no standing ovation. Besides, I was tired and out of breath. I hadn't worked like that in a long time. I did so many handshakes that night I thought my hand was going to fall off. I was sweating and trying to figure out what just happened. People were saying all kinds of stuff.

"Sylvia. That was the bomb! You kilt it!"

"Hey Sylvia – I ain't seen you! Where you been. Girl, you still got it!"

A male stripper named Total Package came by and gave me thumbs up. Chris said "See! I told ya!"

I met a guy named Tracey Jackson who told me about several rooms. Wayne Manigo booked me for his room at a place called Recessions. The night at Recessions I saw Wayne pointing at me telling people I was coming on soon and they needed to watch me. He had to be kidding. My good friend Kitty Behan showed up. I almost cried when I saw her. It was a great room and a great crowd.

By then my friends list was up to 500. I couldn't believe I had 500 friends on Facebook! I was going to a room every night getting on the stage and performing. If you had an open mike room, I was showing up. I knew that the secret to getting good was to get on stage as much as you could and refine whatever it is you were doing. I sometimes did 2 or 3 comedy rooms per night. I couldn't help but reflect on how many rooms they had today as opposed to back in the day. I had no problems getting stage time. Already the chatter about Sylvia was growing.

I went to Martini's one night because Teddy Carpenter, a well known comic from the DMV took over the hosting job from Chris. I walked in, sat in a front seat and watched the show. Teddy kept watching me but for some reason could not place my face. I hadn't seen him since one night at

Mr. Henrys in the Adams Morgan area of DC. Martin Lawrence was doing open mike as was David Reavis. Chris Paul, who is now working with Huggy Lowdown was there. I remember getting off the stage and Chris Paul telling me that Teddy likes me and might use me for some of his shows. I never heard back from either one.

Another night at Martini's there was this girl who was performing. She was fearless on stage, said anything and could care less what anyone thought. I said to myself, OMG, this girl is unbelievable and will do anything. I had a gut feeling that she was going to do something big in the comedy field. Joncea Dixon did not play.

I was meeting all kinds of comics. Chris Thomas had more work for me than I could imagine. My set was up to 20 minutes. Coco Brown was coming to town to headline. Eddie Bryant, the guy behind the success at Club Elite's LOL asked if I wanted to feature for her. Eddie was very particular about who he hired for the club so I figured it was an honor to be asked. I couldn't wait to see Coco because I'd heard so much about her, and true to the word, she was wonderful.

I met Shep, a lesbian comedian. She was excellent. Matty Abrams was adorable and so was Jessica Brodkin. I met her for the first time with Hillary Buckholtz at a Comedy Supreme Show hosted by Virginia's Adaylah Banks. She hired me to headline her first 2 shows. They were packed and full of fun.

After that, I started getting calls for private engagements for parties. The local comedy club rooms hosted by my comedy colleagues were calling me to headline in their rooms. Chico, who I thought was one of the funniest guys in the DMV started hosting Martini's. He asked me to do his room for Women's Month. I was there the last Tuesday that March to a standing room only crowd. People wanted to see what all the chatter was about.

I met a guy named Tony Stewart Spoon whose writing was nothing short of brilliant. He was, in my opinion, a master.

Chris started hiring me to feature with some of what he considered the best comics in the DMV. He put me on a show with Timmy Hall, a comic/Baltimore cop. This guy was hilarious. Next thing I knew I was working with Kevin Lee, the best juggler/show comic I knew, who I hadn't seen in years and a guy named Larry Lancaster who lots of people talked about. I couldn't wait to see him and oh was he funny! He lived up to his reputation.

A group named Laffs on the Harbor was coming to town. One of the guys in charge, Bob Sumner, from Russell Simmon's Def Comedy Jam was bringing Red Grant, Ray Grady, Davian Velez and Corey Fernandez to Bobby McKeys. A comedienne, Raydiva Oneal was hosting the new comic portion and Chris was standing in for Mike Brooks, one of DC's favorites from the Donnie Simpson Show on WPGC. The place was packed. Before I could get in the door good, Chris asked Bob Sumner about putting me on stage. "Bob, you gotta see this girl. She does impressions." Bob told Chris the stage was his and do what he wants. I will always remember that moment with Chris Thomas. He used his celebrity to put me on that stage with no questions asked.

Chris also took me to the House of Chang where another female comic, Gee Gee Wong was hosting. She let me go up for a few minutes. I met all kinds of comics.

Next thing I knew I was developing a family in Baltimore thanks to Raydiva. I met Kleon the Comedian, Frank Nitty and a few others. They were hiring me in their rooms and my schedule was getting crazy. Some weekends I was hired to do 2 or 3 shows each night.

I met Queen Aisha who is a DMV favorite and seemed to be everywhere. Alycia Cooper who wrote for the Parkers and was on all kinds of national shows, invited me to work her room as her headliner. I was so busy I almost didn't have time to breathe.

Michael Black, Danny Rolando, Chip Jones and Ed Blaze were everywhere. They were local comics who were on a grind.

Comics were forming groups so that if you hired one person, you'd luck up and get three. There was CGM with Vernell Simon, Ms. MeMe and Khai Morgan. There was the Misfitz with Henry Jonez, Ms. Aisha Gunn and Marcia Jones from out of Baltimore.

I heard all of this hoopla about a guy named T.L. Fitz who worked a lot with L'il Troy Lamont! One night I did an open mike with Lamont King, another DC favorite who use to be on the radio with Russ Parr in the morning. Not only had Lamont never heard of me, he never saw me perform. He laughed when I was done and said, "I have to go up behind that?" I was honored because Lamont holds his own.

Before I knew it, comics were saying I was their mentor. They had a lot of respect for my history. I started hearing the term "Civil Rights Mother of Comedy." It was nuts!

I remember one night a new comic named Jerone Lyda-El asked if I had time to watch his set and give him my opinion. I wondered to myself, why would he care what I thought? He later told me that it was important for him to know. I laughed to myself, thinking, really? I learned that this guy was serious about his craft and took to heart whatever he learned. If given advice, he took it and ran with it.

Wayne and I put together a comedy conference held in Irwin Loring's comedy room in Maryland. I lucked up and got Jeff Penn, who I hadn't seen since our Star Search auditions, and Tracey Longo to speak. Jim Bell did the legal part of the conference and John Herr who was called Herricane did a bit at the end. John and Fred Rivers supported everybody's room. Brian Kerns was making a big name for himself as was Adam Dodd.

By this time I had a good 45 minutes of solid good clean comedy. The churches started coming after me to entertain their establishments and programs. Next thing I knew I was called to come to Houston to do a show with Marcus D. Wiley and Yolanda Adams. That show touched my heart because although completely different, Yolanda's gospel celebrity reminded me of Whitney Houston to a degree. It's been a whirlwind ever since.

I started traveling to other cities, learning of other comics. The more and more I ventured out, the more it became clear to me that being a comic is an incredible job. However, it wasn't until a woman by the name of Laurinda Boyd said and reminded me. "You're not a comic Sylvia. You're an entertainer." That rang true for me.

I thought about the journey I had back in the day, when I was traveling by myself, hungry for a microphone, pressed to get on stage and hoping for an opportunity. Remembering how there were no other Black women hitting those D.C., Los Angeles and New York pavements with me. Those days are over. It's a different time and place. Although I'm still faced with adversity there's a big difference between now and then. The beauty of it for me is I'm back. I'm working, I'm thankful, I'm blessed and I'm delighted. What a journey!

I hope you've enjoyed the reading. It's been one heck of a time and as you can see, I was Almost There, Almost.

May God always bring you peace.

ABOUT THE AUTHOR

Sylvia Traymore Morrison is currently enjoying touring with Almost There, Almost, speaking and performing at venues that highlight domestic violence, HIV/AIDS and entertainment and comedy. She is currently prepping for a one woman show entitled Almost There, Almost. Please visit www.syivlatraymore.com for updates.

Made in the USA
Charleston, SC
02 December 2011